스토리가 있는
카툰 영단어
발행일   2013년 7월 5일

지은이	최지혜, 신희영
발행인	김태웅
총 괄	권혁주
책임편집	최지향
디자인	최진화
마케팅	서재욱, 김흥태, 정상석, 장영임
	이규태, 김귀찬, 왕성석, 김철영
제 작	현대순

발행처	동양북스
등 록	제 10-806호(1993년 4월 3일)
주 소	서울시 마포구 서교동 463-16호 (121-842)
전 화	02-337-1737
팩 스	02-334-6624
홈페이지	http://www.dongyangbooks.com

ISBN 978-89-98914-25-7   13740

▶ 본 책은 저작권법에 의해 보호를 받는 저작물이므로 무단 전재와 복제를 금합니다.
▶ 잘못된 책은 구입처에서 교환해 드립니다.

스토리가 있는 카투영단어

당당하게 어학연수 떠나는 스토리 영단어

최지혜·신희영 지음

Preface

영어 단어 암기는 영어를 배우는 사람들의 영원한 숙제인 것 같습니다. 특히 시험에서 좋은 점수를 받기 위해 지루한 단어리스트를 암기하는 과정, 모두 겪어보셨을 겁니다. 하지만 뇌가 가장 싫어하는 것이 지루한 반복 학습이라고 하죠? 그래서인지 요즘은 나날이 새로운 영어 암기 비법이 개발되고 있습니다. 그럼에도 불구하고 정말 편하게 단어를 익히는 방법을 찾기란 쉽지 않더군요. 그에 대한 끊임없는 고민과 연구 끝에 이 영어 단어 교재를 개발하게 되었습니다.

우리는 영어 단어 책을 볼 때 다음과 같은 두 가지 의문을 가지게 됩니다. 첫 번째는 바로 '여기 나오는 단어들이 내게 꼭 필요한 단어들인가?'입니다. 이 교재에는 현재 대한민국에서 가장 대표적인 공인시험인 토익, 토플, 텝스, 니트의 필수 어휘만을 선별하여 담았습니다. 다양한 시험에 공통으로 나오는 단어인 만큼, 실제 영어를 사용할 때도 필수적인 단어들입니다. 즉, 이 단어들을 공부함으로써 시험 점수가 오르는 것은 물론 영어 신문이나 방송 같은 콘텐츠를 접할 때도 많은 도움을 받을 수 있습니다.

두 번째는 '이 책을 통해 효과적으로 단어를 배울 수 있을까?'일 것입니다. 우리는 지금까지의 경험을 통해서 학습의 과정이 재미있을수록 그 결과 또한 효과적이라는 것을 알고 있습니다. 그래서 이 교재의 목표를 '꼭 필요한 단어를 더 쉽게, 더 재미있게 학습하기'로 잡았습니다. 그럼 가장 쉬운, 가장 재미있는 학습 방법은 어떤 것일까요? 여러 연구 결과들은 암기하고자 하는 대상에 연상할 수 있는 의미를 덧붙이는 것을 그 비법으로 제시하고 있습니다. 의미를 붙이는 가장 효과적인 방법의 하나는 재미있는 이야기와 결합시키는 것입니다. 사람들은 항상 누군가의 이야기에 귀를 기울이게 되기 때문입니다. 여기에 그림이 더해진다면 그 효과는 배가 되겠죠? 이 책은 주인공인 Allie가 영국에서 실제로 겪었던 다양한 일화를 카툰으로 각색하여 단어와 함께 전달하고 있습니다.

Allie의 이야기에 귀를 기울여 주세요! 그러면 절대로 안 외워지던 영어 단어들이 자연스럽게 머릿속에 저장되는 즐거운 경험을 하실 수 있을 것입니다. 학습자들께서 재미와 정보, 영어 단어 학습이라는 세 마리 토끼를 모두 잡을 수 있기를 바랍니다.

최지혜, 신희영

About this book

카툰을 통해 단어를 쉽고 재미있게 학습!

카툰 캐릭터들의 대화 속에 목표 단어만 영어로 제시되어 재미있게 단어의 의미를 추측해 볼 수 있습니다. 이런 과정은 해당 단어에 관한 관심을 높이는 촉매제 역할을 하면서 더 효과적인 단어 습득이 이루어지도록 도움을 줍니다.

다양한 상식과 정보의 습득!

이 책의 가장 큰 장점은 이야기를 통해 영어 단어를 학습할 수 있다는 것입니다. 영국 런던을 배경으로 실제 경험을 바탕으로 한 생생한 이야기를 따라가다 보면, 단어를 자연스럽게 접하면서 유용한 정보와 상식도 함께 배울 수 있습니다.

자연스러운 일상 회화까지 정복!

카툰으로 읽은 한국어 대화들은 영어 문장을 통해 다시 한 번 학습이 가능합니다. 최대한 자연스러운 구어체 형식의 문장을 제시함으로써 단순한 단어 학습을 넘어 직접적인 회화 실력 향상도 기대할 수 있습니다.

다양한 단어 학습 장치 제공!

교재의 목표 단어를 총 7단계(Preview, 카툰, 단어 정의, 연어, 예문, 연습 문제, 번역문)의 반복을 통해 학습함으로써 장기 기억으로 저장될 수 있는 확률을 높입니다. 또한, 추가로 유의어 및 파생어를 함께 제시함으로써 단어의 의미를 좀 더 명확하게 이해할 수 있습니다.

1. 학습 방법

이 교재는 20일 완성 코스로 기획되었습니다. 아래의 방법을 따라 매일 한 단원(Day)씩 학습하시기 바랍니다.

2. 진도 체크

교재를 완료하기까지의 목표 일수와 실제 학습 일수를 기록하여 비교할 수 있습니다. 한 Day를 끝낼 때마다 아래의 빈칸에 완료 표시(○), 혹은 학습한 날짜를 기록하면서 진도를 체크합니다.

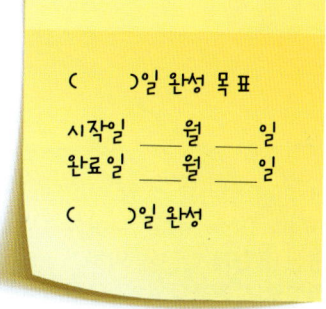

Day 1	Day 2	Day 3	Day 4	Day 5
Day 6	Day 7	Day 8	Day 9	Day 10
Day 11	Day 12	Day 13	Day 14	Day 15
Day 16	Day 17	Day 18	Day 19	Day 20

Construction

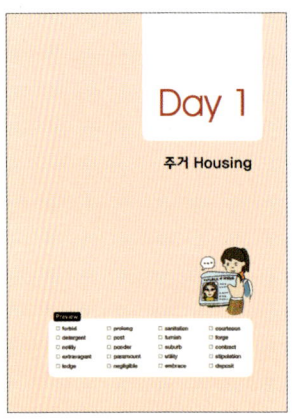

Preview

이 단원에서 학습할 단어들을 한눈에 보여주고 있습니다. 이미 알고 있는 단어들은 체크해보고, 모르는 단어들은 눈으로 익히면서 본격적인 단어 학습을 준비해봅니다.

카툰 이야기

주인공 Allie와 친구들이 영국 생활과 재미있는 정보를 영어 단어와 함께 보여주는 코너입니다. 편한 마음으로 내용을 이해하면서 영어 단어의 뜻을 추측해 보세요.

단어 리스트

목표 단어와의 관련 학습을 통해 단어 확장이 가능합니다. 또한, 목표 단어가 주로 쓰이는 중심 표현과 예문을 익히면서 단어를 효과적으로 활용할 수 있도록 해보세요.

단어 뜻 연습문제

단어의 정의와 카툰을 통해 제시된 문장을 활용해 목표 단어를 연습해보는 코너입니다. 앞의 이야기들을 떠올리며 단어의 의미를 찾아보세요.

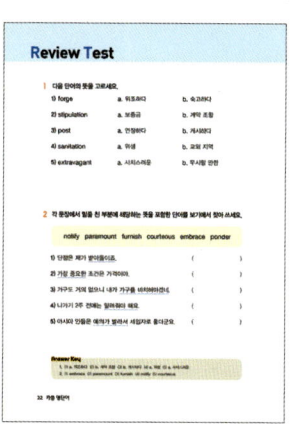

유의어 및 예문 연습문제

앞서 학습한 파생어와 유의어들을 목표 단어와 함께 제시한 문제들입니다. 보기로 제시된 단어들도 잊지 말고 다시 한 번 의미를 체크해보세요.

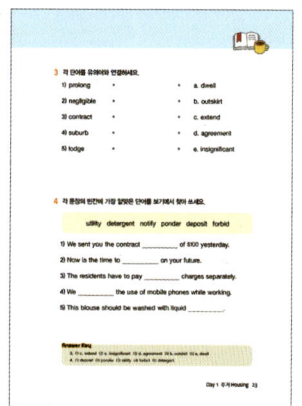

카툰 번역문

각 Unit에서 한글로 제시되었던 대화들의 영어 번역 문장들입니다. 이 문장들을 잘 활용하면 영어 문장을 만드는데도 자신감이 붙을 수 있겠죠?

Contents

Day 1   주거 Housing ························· 13
홈스테이 / 좀 더 싼 방으로 / 허름한 1인실 / 내 얼굴 맞아요

Day 2   직업 Job ························· 25
일자리 구하기 / 우연한 행운 / 참 쉽죠 / 직장이 다 그렇지

Day 3   만남 Encounter ························· 37
예쁜걸 / 봉사단체 / 잘생겼군요 / 카부츠 벼룩시장의 그녀

Day 4   쇼핑 Shopping ························· 49
차이나타운 / 우산은 필수 / 가구가 필요해 / 자선가게에서의 쇼핑

Day 5   건강 Health ························· 61
전염되나요 / 환경이 안 좋아 / 영양 결핍 / 왕여드름을 달고

Day 6   일상 Daily Life ························· 73
초여름의 꿈 / 픽업아티스트 / 운명의 장난 / 희망찬 해외취업

Day 7   경험 Experience ························· 85
런던 날씨는 예측 불가 / 밤의 정원 / 하늘을 날고 싶어 / 어차피 남의 인연

Day 8   인생 Life ························· 97
함께 살자 / 유대인의 결혼 / 캐롤의 아버지 / 엄마의 전화

Day 9   현실 Reality ························· 109
충동구매 자제 / 담장 너머 / 추억을 잃다 / 소원해진 관계

Day 10   위기 Cricis ························· 121
아이의 발언 / 마이너스 통장 / 보따리 장사 / 도둑이야

Day 11   사건 Incident —————————————— 133
희롱당했어 / 불합리한 판결 / 충격과 분노 / 위로의 스튜

Day 12   여행 Travel ———————————————— 145
모니카의 고향으로 / 시스티나 성당 / 관람객 주의사항 / 사라져가는 도시

Day 13   학교 School ———————————————— 157
다시 일상으로 / 대영제국 / 나를 봐 줘 / 토론 주제

Day 14   경제 Economy ————————————— 169
어수선한 사회 / 복지정책 / 우리나라 제품인데 / 이상과 현실

Day 15   전쟁 War ————————————————— 181
크림전쟁 / 나이팅게일 / 의료체계의 개혁 / 메리 시콜

Day 16   문학·예술 Arts ———————————— 193
오리엔트 특급 살인 / 외로운 괴물 / 트리스탄과 이졸데 / 거리미술가

Day 17   역사 History ———————————————— 205
리즈 캐슬 / 퀸 엘리자베스 / 운명의 수레바퀴 / 국기의 유래

Day 18   전통 Tradition ——————————————— 217
할로윈 의상 / 가이 포크스 데이 / 크리스마스 손님 / 새해 키스는 누구와

Day 19   교육 Education ——————————————— 229
드라마는 자막 없이 / 스파르타 학원 / 학비를 모아요 / 비자 연장

Day 20   미래 Future ———————————————— 241
딸은 아버지를 닮아간다 / 아직은 정착이 싫은 / 모니카의 꿈 / 앨리의 미래

Characters

Allie
어학연수생
일과 공부를 병행 중

Yang
아르바이트 동료
착한 마음씨를
가진 중국인

Carol
영국인 친구
Allie의 현지
생활을 도와 줌

Monica
어학원 동기
디자인 전공의
이탈리아 인

Julio
어학원 동기
넘치는 매력의
스페인 청년

Chef Jang
한국인 요리사
성공을 꿈꾸며
해외로 취업

Day 1

주거 Housing

Preview

- ☐ forbid
- ☐ detergent
- ☐ notify
- ☐ extravagant
- ☐ lodge
- ☐ prolong
- ☐ post
- ☐ ponder
- ☐ paramount
- ☐ negligible
- ☐ sanitation
- ☐ furnish
- ☐ suburb
- ☐ utility
- ☐ embrace
- ☐ courteous
- ☐ forge
- ☐ contract
- ☐ stipulation
- ☐ deposit

Unit 01 홈스테이

LET'S STUDY

forbid
[fərbíd]
⑤ 금지하다

▶ forbidden
⑧ 금지된

forbid the use of ~의 사용을 금지하다
forbid the sale of ~의 판매를 금지하다

We forbid the use of mobile phones while working.
일하는 동안 휴대폰 사용을 금지한다.
The laws of our country forbid the sale of hard drugs.
우리나라의 법은 중독성 마약의 판매를 금지한다.

detergent
[ditə́ːrdʒənt]
⑲ 세제
⑧ 세척하는

▶ deterge
⑤ 세척하다

laundry **detergent** 세탁용 세제
liquid **detergent** 액상 세제

Karen asked her brother to buy laundry detergent.
카렌은 남동생에게 세탁용 세제를 사오라고 부탁했다.
This blouse should be washed with liquid detergent.
이 블라우스는 액상용 세제로 세탁해야 한다.

notify
[nóutəfài]
⑤ 알리다, 신고하다

▶ notice
⑲ 공지
⑤ 알아차리다

notify parents of ~을 부모님에게 알리다
notify the police of ~을 경찰에게 신고하다

The school notified all the parents of the new program.
학교는 그 새 프로그램에 대해 모든 부모님들께 알렸다.
I will notify the police of the crime scene.
나는 범죄현장을 경찰에게 신고할 것이다.

extravagant
[ikstrǽvəgənt]
⑧ 사치스러운, 낭비하는
(= wasteful)

an **extravagant** gift 사치스러운 선물
an **extravagant** wedding 사치스러운 결혼식

My uncle gave me a rather extravagant gift.
삼촌께서 내게 다소 사치스러운 선물을 주셨다.
Jack and Molly plan to have an extravagant wedding.
잭과 몰리는 사치스러운 결혼식을 할 계획이다.

lodge
[ladʒ]
⑤ 거주하다(= dwell);
남다(= remain)
⑲ 오두막집(= cabin)

lodge in a hotel 호텔에 묵다
lodge in mind 마음에 남다

Emma lodged in a luxurious hotel on her trip to Paris.
에마는 파리 여행 중에 호화로운 호텔에서 묵었다.
All the details of the story lodged in my mind.
그 이야기의 모든 세부사항들이 내 마음에 남았다.

Unit 02 좀더 싼 방으로

더 이상 홈스테이 생활을 **prolong**할 수는 없겠어.

나처럼 싼 방 찾는 손님은 중개업자가 별로 안 반기겠지?

post된 광고들로 내가 **ponder**해 봐야겠다.

paramount 조건은 가격이야.

다른 문제들은 **negligible**이지.

1인실이면 좋겠지만 아무래도 무리일 듯.

LET'S STUDY

prolong
[prəlɔ́(ː)ŋ]
⑧ 연장하다(= extend)

prolong stay 체류 기간을 연장하다
prolong life 수명을 연장하다

I want to prolong my stay in this city.
나는 이 도시에서의 체류기간을 연장하고 싶다.
This new treatment might be able to prolong my life.
이 새로운 치료법이 내 수명을 연장시킬 수도 있다.

post
[poust]
⑧ 게시하다(= put);
  발송하다(= send)
⑲ 게시물; 우편(= mail)

post an ad 광고를 게시하다
post a picture 사진을 올리다

I posted an ad on the board to sell my used car.
중고차를 팔기 위해 게시판에 광고를 게시했다.
Jenny posted several pictures of the party online.
제니는 그 파티의 사진 여러 개를 인터넷에 올렸다.

ponder
[pándər]
⑧ 숙고하다, 깊이 생각하다
  (= speculate)

ponder on a problem 그 문제에 대해 숙고하다
ponder on future 미래에 대해 숙고하다

Jack has been pondering on the problem.
잭은 그 문제에 대해 숙고해 왔다.
Now is the time to ponder on your future.
지금이 네 미래에 대해 숙고해야 할 때이다.

paramount
[pǽrəmàunt]
⑱ 가장 중요한(= vital)

a paramount concern 가장 중요한 관심사
a paramount role 가장 중요한 역할

My paramount concern is the safety of everyone.
내 가장 큰 관심사는 모두의 안전이다.
The paramount role of parents is to love their kids.
부모의 가장 중요한 역할은 자녀를 사랑하는 것이다.

negligible
[néɡlidʒəbl]
⑱ 무시할 만한, 사소한
  (= insignificant)

a negligible amount 무시할 만한 양
a negligible difference 사소한 차이

This tea contains a negligible amount of caffeine.
이 차는 무시할 만한 양의 카페인을 포함하고 있다.
There is only a negligible difference between them.
그것들 사이에는 아주 사소한 차이만 있다.

Unit 03

허름한 1인실

LET'S STUDY

sanitation
[sǽnitéiʃən]
명 위생, 위생 시설

a **sanitation** condition 위생 상태
a **sanitation** worker 환경 미화원

Sanitation conditions in our building are excellent.
우리 건물의 위생 상태는 매우 훌륭하다.
The streets are clean thanks to sanitation workers.
환경 미화원분들 덕분에 거리가 깨끗하다.

---

furnish
[fə́:rniʃ]
동 가구를 비치하다
(=decorate);
제공하다(= supply)

furnish a room 방에 가구를 비치하다
furnish an apartment 아파트에 가구를 비치하다

I really should go shopping to furnish my new room.
새 방에 가구를 비치하기 위해 정말 쇼핑을 해야겠다.
It costs a lot of money to furnish an apartment.
아파트에 가구를 비치하는 것은 3많은 돈이 든다.

---

suburb
[sʌ́bəːrb]
명 교외 지역, 근교
(= outskirt)

a **suburb** of ~의 교외 지역
a residential **suburb** of ~의 교외 주택 지역

Sarah moved to a suburb of London after marriage.
사라는 결혼 후에 런던 교외 지역으로 이사했다.
I live in a residential suburb of New York.
나는 뉴욕의 교외 주택 지역에 산다.

---

utility
[ju:tíləti]
명 공익사업
(= public service);
유용(= usefulness)
형 다용도의

utility charges 공공요금
an electric **utility** company 전력 공급 회사

The residents have to pay utility charges separately.
입주자들은 공공요금을 각자 지불해야 한다.
You have to contact your electric utility company.
너는 전력 공급 회사에 연락해야 한다.

---

embrace
[imbréis]
동 받아들이다(= accept)

embrace demerits 단점을 받아들이다
embrace destiny 운명을 받아들이다

Jenny decided to embrace the demerits of her job.
제니는 그녀의 직업이 가진 단점들을 받아들이기로 했다.
I'm finally ready to embrace my destiny.
나는 마침내 내 운명을 받아들일 준비가 되었다.

Unit 04 내 얼굴 맞아요

LET'S STUDY

courteous
[kə́ːrtiəs]
- 형 예의 바른, 공손한
- ▶ courteously
  - 부 공손하게

courteous behavior 예의 바른 행동
a courteous service 예의 바른 서비스

I was really impressed by his courteous behavior.
나는 그의 예의 바른 행동에 깊이 감명받았다.
This hotel is well known for its courteous service.
이 호텔은 예의 바른 서비스로 유명하다.

---

forge
[fɔːrdʒ]
- 동 위조하다; 맺다
- ▶ forgery
  - 명 위조

forge a signature 사인을 위조하다
forge a relationship 관계를 맺다

Jake is an expert in forging a signature.
제이크는 사인을 위조하는 것에 전문가이다.
I hope that we can forge a good relationship.
우리가 좋은 관계를 맺을 수 있기를 희망한다.

---

contract
[kántrækt]
- 명 계약서, 계약
  (= agreement)
- 동 계약하다 [kəntrǽkt]

sign a contract 계약서에 사인하다
break a contract 계약을 깨다

Once you sign the contract, you belong to our firm.
그 계약서에 사인을 하면, 당신은 우리 회사 소속이 된다.
If you break the contract, there will be consequences.
당신이 계약을 깨면, 그에 따른 결과가 있을 것이다.

---

stipulation
[stìpjuléiʃən]
- 명 계약 조항
- ▶ stipulate
  - 동 규정하다

agree to the stipulation 계약 조항에 동의하다
a stipulation in a contract 계약서 내의 조항

I will sell you this one if you agree to this stipulation.
이 계약 조항에 동의한다면 이것을 너에게 팔 것이다.
I'd like to change one stipulation in the contract.
나는 계약서 내의 조항 하나를 바꾸고 싶다.

---

deposit
[dipázit]
- 명 보증금; 예금
- 동 예금하다 (= save)

a contract deposit 계약 보증금
deposit money 돈을 예금하다

We sent you the contract deposit of $100 yesterday.
우리는 어제 당신에게 계약 보증금 100달러를 보냈다.
I deposit money in my bank account every Monday.
나는 매주 월요일에 내 계좌에 돈을 예금한다.

Review Test

1 다음 단어의 뜻을 고르세요.

1) forge   a. 위조하다   b. 숙고하다

2) stipulation   a. 보증금   b. 계약 조항

3) post   a. 연장하다   b. 게시하다

4) sanitation   a. 위생   b. 교외 지역

5) extravagant   a. 사치스러운   b. 무시할 만한

2 각 문장에서 밑줄 친 부분에 해당하는 뜻을 포함한 단어를 보기에서 찾아 쓰세요.

> notify   paramount   furnish   courteous   embrace   ponder

1) 단점은 제가 <u>받아들이죠</u>.   (   )

2) <u>가장 중요한</u> 조건은 가격이야.   (   )

3) 가구도 거의 없으니 내가 <u>가구를 비치해야</u>겠네. (   )

4) 나가기 2주 전에는 <u>알려줘야</u> 해요.   (   )

5) 아시아 인들은 <u>예의가 발라서</u> 세입자로 좋더군요. (   )

Answer Key

1. (1) a. 위조하다 (2) b. 계약 조항 (3) b. 게시하다 (4) a. 위생 (5) a. 사치스러운
2. (1) embrace (2) paramount (3) furnish (4) notify (5) courteous

3 각 단어를 유의어와 연결하세요.

1) prolong •   • a. dwell

2) negligible •   • b. outskirt

3) contract •   • c. extend

4) suburb •   • d. agreement

5) lodge •   • e. insignificant

4 각 문장의 빈칸에 가장 알맞은 단어를 보기에서 찾아 쓰세요.

> utility   detergent   notify   ponder   deposit   forbid

1) We sent you the contract _____ of $100 yesterday.

2) Now is the time to _____ on your future.

3) The residents have to pay _____ charges separately.

4) We _____ the use of mobile phones while working.

5) This blouse should be washed with liquid _____.

Answer Key

3. (1) c. extend (2) e. insignificant (3) d. agreement (4) b. outskirt (5) a. dwell
4. (1) deposit (2) ponder (3) utility (4) forbid (5) detergent

Let's Speak

Unit 1

Woman I forbid you to bring your friends home. Next to the washing machine is a bottle of laundry detergent, and you can use it freely. If you want to move out, you have to notify me 2 weeks in advance.

Allie (The owner looks friendly, and it would be convenient to live here. Doing a home-stay would feel too extravagant for me. Maybe I should lodge here for just a short time and then move out to a flat.) I rushed into coming here without enough savings.

Unit 2

Allie I can't prolong my stay in this place. (I bet realtors do not like customers like me who are looking for cheap places. I have to study the posted ads and ponder over this problem. Price is the paramount concern for me. The other matters are negligible. I want to live in a single room, but that's not likely to happen.)

Unit 3

Allie (Sanitation here is terribly poor. Since there is hardly any furniture, I need to furnish the room. This is a suburb of London, far from the language school.)

Man I know what you are thinking, but utility charges are also included in the rent. And this is the cheapest single room in this area.

Allie I'll take it. I will embrace the demerits!

Unit 4

Man Asians are good tenants since they are courteous. You didn't forge your passport, did you?

Allie I am wearing make-up in the photo.

Man Well, I guess I have to trust you. Sign the contract.

Allie What is this payment for in this stipulation?

Man This is the deposit that you pay when you rent a room. Don't worry. You'll get it back when you move out.

Day 2

직업 Job

Preview

- ☐ successive
- ☐ district
- ☐ vacancy
- ☐ exhausted
- ☐ overcome
- ☐ resident
- ☐ coincidence
- ☐ recruit
- ☐ consent
- ☐ unanimous
- ☐ supervise
- ☐ mandatory
- ☐ dull
- ☐ readily
- ☐ fragile
- ☐ sluggish
- ☐ kin
- ☐ exploit
- ☐ monetary
- ☐ conscience

Unit 01 일자리 구하기

LET'S STUDY

successive
[səksésiv]
형 연속된, 계속된

▶ successively
  부 연속적으로
▶ successiveness
  명 연속

successive games 연속된 경기
successive years 연속된 연도

Our soccer team has won 3 successive games.
우리 축구 팀이 세 경기 연속으로 이겼다.
I have won this competition for 5 successive years.
나는 이 대회를 5년 연속으로 우승했다.

---

district
[dístrikt]
명 지역, 지방(= region)

a shopping **district** 쇼핑 지역
a **district** attorney 지방 검사

The shopping district is almost empty now.
지금은 쇼핑 지역이 거의 텅 비어 있다.
The district attorney will call you within a week.
지방 검사가 일주일 안에 너에게 전화를 할 것이다.

---

vacancy
[véikənsi]
명 빈자리, 가능한 자리

▶ vacant
  형 비어 있는

fill a **vacancy** 빈자리를 채우다
a **vacancy** rate 공석률

I hope we find the right person to fill the vacancy.
그 자리를 채울 적임자를 우리가 찾을 수 있기를 바란다.
Apartment vacancy rates keep rising in this town.
이 도시의 아파트 공석률이 계속 올라간다.

---

exhausted
[igzɔ́:stid]
형 매우 지친, 녹초가 된

▶ exhaustion
  명 피로, 고갈
▶ exhaust
  명 배출
  동 녹초가 되게 하다

be physically **exhausted** 신체적으로 매우 지치다
be mentally **exhausted** 정신적으로 매우 지치다

Olivia was physically exhausted after a long flight.
올리비아는 긴 비행 후에 신체적으로 매우 지쳤다.
I was mentally exhausted after the test.
나는 그 시험 이후에 정신적으로 매우 지쳤다.

---

overcome
[òuvərkʌ́m]
동 극복하다, 이겨내다
  (= withstand)

overcome hardships 어려움을 극복하다
overcome differences 차이를 극복하다

I'll overcome hardships to ensure my future success.
나는 미래의 성공을 위해 어려움을 극복해 낼 것이다.
We overcame our differences and got married.
우리는 서로의 차이를 극복하고 결혼했다.

Unit 02 우연한 행운

LET'S STUDY

resident
[rézidənt]
명 거주자, 주민

▶ residence
  명 주소, 거주지

a former **resident** 이전 거주자
a lifelong **resident** 평생 동안의 거주자

The former resident of this room was my friend.
이 방의 이전 거주자는 내 친구였다.
My grandfather is a lifelong resident of this city.
할아버지께서는 이 도시에서 평생 사신 분이다.

---

coincidence
[kouínsidəns]
명 우연의 일치

▶ coincident
  형 일치하는
▶ coincide
  동 일치하다

a pure **coincidence** 완전한 우연의 일치
a strange **coincidence** 기묘한 우연의 일치

By pure coincidence, John and I met here again.
완전한 우연의 일치로 존과 나는 여기서 다시 만났다.
Our relationship started with a strange coincidence.
우리의 관계는 기묘한 우연의 일치로 시작되었다.

---

recruit
[rikrú:t]
동 모집하다, 채용하다
명 신입

▶ recruitment
  명 채용, 신규 모집

recruit volunteers 자원봉사자를 모집하다
recruit new members 새 회원을 모집하다

I need to recruit quite a few volunteers for this event.
나는 이 행사를 위해서 많은 자원봉사자들을 모집해야 한다.
The book club is recruiting new members.
그 독서회는 새 회원들을 모집하는 중이다.

---

consent
[kənsént]
명 동의, 허락(= approval)
동 동의하다

a **consent** to marriage 결혼 동의
a **consent** form 동의서

My father didn't give his consent to my marriage.
아버지께서는 내 결혼에 동의하지 않으셨다.
You need to sign this consent form now.
너는 지금 이 동의서에 사인해야 한다.

---

unanimous
[ju:nǽnəməs]
형 만장일치의

▶ unanimity
  명 만장일치
▶ unanimously
  부 만장일치로

a **unanimous** decision 만장일치의 결정
a **unanimous** vote 만장일치의 표

It was a unanimous decision that we hire you.
당신을 고용하는 것은 만장일치의 결정이었다.
The proposal was approved by a unanimous vote.
그 제안은 만장일치의 표로 채택되었다.

Unit 03 참 쉽죠

LET'S STUDY

supervise
[sjú:pərvàiz]
ⓥ 관리하다, 감독하다
(= manage)

supervise employees 직원들을 관리하다
supervise a project 프로젝트를 총괄하다

I'll teach you how to supervise employees effectively.
내가 너에게 직원들을 효과적으로 관리하는 방법을 가르쳐줄 것이다.
Emma is in charge of supervising this project.
엠마는 이 프로젝트의 총괄 책임을 맡고 있다.

mandatory
[mǽndətɔ̀:ri]
ⓐ 의무적인, 강제적인
(= compulsory)

a **mandatory** sentence 의무 복역
a **mandatory** meeting 의무적인 회의

Sam received a mandatory sentence of 10 years.
샘은 10년의 의무 복역을 선고받았다.
I couldn't make the mandatory meeting this morning.
나는 오늘 아침에 열린 의무적인 회의에 참석하지 못했다.

dull
[dʌl]
ⓐ 지루한(= boring);
무딘(= blunt)
ⓥ 둔하게 하다

a **dull** life 지루한 인생
a **dull** knife 무딘 칼

I had led a dull life before meeting her.
나는 그녀를 만나기 전에는 지루한 삶을 살았다.
You can't cut carrots with such a dull knife.
그런 무딘 칼로는 당근을 자를 수 없다.

readily
[rédəli]
ⓐ 쉽게(= effortlessly);
기꺼이(= gladly)

readily available 쉽게 가능한
readily admit 기꺼이 인정하다

Internet access is readily available in each room.
인터넷 접속이 각 방에서 쉽게 가능하다.
Stella readily admitted that what she did was wrong.
스텔라는 그녀가 했던 일이 잘못되었음을 기꺼이 인정했다.

fragile
[frǽdʒəl]
ⓐ 깨지기 쉬운, 연약한
(= brittle)

a **fragile** peace 깨지기 쉬운 평화
emotionally **fragile** 정서적으로 연약한

We have been maintaining a fragile peace.
우리는 깨지기 쉬운 평화를 유지하고 있다.
James is an emotionally fragile person.
제임스는 정서적으로 연약한 사람이다.

Unit 04 직장이 다 그렇지

LET'S STUDY

sluggish
[slʌ́giʃ]
혱 느린(= slow)

at a **sluggish** pace 느린 속도로
a **sluggish** economy 침체된 경기

The sales are increasing at a sluggish pace.
판매량이 느린 속도로 늘어나고 있다.
We are suffering from the sluggish economy.
우리는 침체된 경기 때문에 고통받고 있다.

---

kin
[kin]
혱 친척, 혈연
(= relation)

next of **kin** 가까운 친척
kin within reach 가까운 곳의 친척

Patrick left a large fortune to his next of kin.
패트릭은 가까운 친척에게 엄청난 유산을 남겼다.
It is good to have kin within reach.
가까운 곳에 친척이 있는 것은 좋은 일이다.

---

exploit
[éksplɔit]
동 착취하다; 이용하다

▶ exploitation
명 착취, 이용

exploit employees 직원들을 착취하다
exploit the law 법을 이용하다

Owen exploited his employees to gain more profit.
오웬은 더 많은 이익을 얻기 위해 직원들을 착취했다.
Some people exploit the law for their own interests.
어떤 사람들은 자신의 이익을 위해 법을 이용한다.

---

monetary
[mánitèri]
혱 금전적인
(= pecuniary)

monetary compensation 금전적인 보상
monetary value 금전적인 가치

We don't expect any monetary compensation.
우리는 금전적인 보상을 전혀 기대하지 않는다.
This ring does not have much monetary value.
이 반지는 금전적인 가치가 크게 없다.

---

conscience
[kánʃəns]
명 양심, 양심의 가책
(= compunction)

a guilty **conscience** 죄책감
freedom of **conscience** 양심의 자유

It's my guilty conscience keeping me awake at night.
나는 죄책감 때문에 밤에 잠들지 못한다.
In this country, we all have freedom of conscience.
이 나라에서는 우리 모두가 양심의 자유를 가지고 있다.

Review Test

1 다음 단어의 뜻을 고르세요.

1) sluggish	a. 느린		b. 지루한
2) coincidence	a. 우연의 일치		b. 양심
3) recruit	a. 관리하다		b. 모집하다
4) monetary	a. 금전적인		b. 지루한
5) consent	a. 친척		b. 동의

2 각 문장에서 밑줄 친 부분에 해당하는 뜻을 포함한 단어를 보기에서 찾아 쓰세요.

> successive exploit unanimous exhausted district mandatory

1) <u>만장일치</u>의 결정이야! (   )

2) 여기는 인력을 너무 <u>착취해</u>. (   )

3) 어, 이 <u>지역</u>에서 처음 보는 중국음식점이네. (   )

4) 항상 유니폼을 입는 게 <u>의무적이야</u>. (   )

5) 30번 <u>연속된</u> 알바 거절이라니. (   )

Answer Key

1. (1) a. 느린 (2) a. 우연의 일치 (3) b. 모집하다 (4) a. 금전적인 (5) b. 동의
2. (1) unanimous (2) exploit (3) district (4) mandatory (5) successive

3 각 단어를 유의어와 연결하세요.

1) kin • • a. effortlessly

2) overcome • • b. manage

3) supervise • • c. relation

4) readily • • d. brittle

5) fragile • • e. withstand

4 각 문장의 빈칸에 가장 알맞은 단어를 보기에서 찾아 쓰세요.

conscience   exhausted   resident   dull   district   vacancy

1) The former _____ of this room was my friend.

2) I was mentally _____ after the test.

3) I hope we find the right person to fill the _____.

4) I had led a(an) _____ life before meeting her.

5) In this country, we all have freedom of _____.

Answer Key
3. (1) c. relation (2) e. withstand (3) b. manage (4) a. effortlessly (5) d. brittle
4. (1) resident (2) exhausted (3) vacancy (4) dull (5) conscience

Let's Speak

Unit 1

Allie	This makes a total of 30 **successive** refusals. (Oh! That place is the first Chinese restaurant I've seen in the **district**. They must be looking for an Asian employee, so they might hire me.) Is there a **vacancy**?
Boss	We only hire Chinese people.
Allie	I'm totally **exhausted**, but I need to **overcome** any hardship to survive here.

Unit 2

Yang	(I guess I've seen her before. Was she a **resident** here?) Hey! Didn't you visit our restaurant looking for a job?
Allie	Oh. Yes, I did.
Yang	What a **coincidence**! We are still **recruiting** employees. Are you still interested? Boss, Let's hire her!
Allie	Really?
Boss	She's not Chinese…
Yang	You gave me your **consent**, right? It's a **unanimous** decision.
Allie	Thanks a lot!

Unit 3

Yang	I'll **supervise** you from now on. It is **mandatory** for you to wear the uniform. First, start with the dishes. You might find it a bit **dull**, but you can **readily** do this. Ah, these glasses are really **fragile**, so please be careful.

Unit 4

Woman	Don't be **sluggish**! Move!
Allie	Who's that?
Yang	She is one of the boss's **kin**. The boss is really **exploiting** us. We often have to work overtime as well.
Allie	But he offers **monetary** compensation for that, right?
Yang	No way! He even takes away our tips.
Allie	Such a shame! He has no **conscience** at all!

Day 3

만남 Encounter

Preview

- emerge
- genuine
- vigorous
- glance
- proximity
- enclose
- assign
- charitable
- merit
- corrupt
- notable
- concede
- continual
- conflict
- flaw
- extent
- barter
- obsolete
- expenditure
- consumption

Unit 01 예쁜걸

LET'S STUDY

emerge
[imə́ːrdʒ]
⑧ 나오다, 나타나다

▶ emergent
　㊗ 나타나는

emerge from a room 방에서 나오다
emerge from shadows 어둠 속에서 나타나다

Naomi saw her father emerging from the room.
나오미는 아버지가 방에서 나오는 것을 보았다.
A guy suddenly emerged from the shadows.
한 남자가 갑자기 어둠 속에서 나타났다.

genuine
[dʒénjuin]
㊗ 진정한(= real);
　진실한(= sincere)

a **genuine** beauty 진정한 미인
a **genuine** feeling 진실한 감정

Grace is a genuine beauty with a talent for singing.
그레이스는 노래에 재능을 가진 진정한 미인이다.
I had a genuine feeling of love for him.
나는 그에게 진실한 사랑의 감정을 가지고 있었다.

vigorous
[víɡərəs]
㊗ 활발한, 활기 있는

▶ vigor
　㊅ 활기
▶ vigorously
　㊉ 활기 있게

a **vigorous** debate 활발한 토론
vigorous exercise 격렬한 운동

We had a vigorous debate about the recycling system.
우리는 재활용 시스템에 관해 활발한 토론을 했다.
You always have to stretch after vigorous exercise.
격렬한 운동 후에는 항상 스트레칭을 해야 한다.

glance
[ɡlæns]
㊅ 힐끗 봄(= glimpse)
⑧ 잠깐 보다(= peek)

at a **glance** 한 눈에
cast a **glance** at ~에 살짝 눈길을 주다

I could tell at a glance that you were a good person.
나는 당신이 좋은 사람임을 한 눈에 알 수 있었다.
Mark cast a glance at the girl next to the door.
마크는 문 옆의 소녀에게 잠시 눈길을 주었다.

proximity
[prɑksíməti]
㊅ 가까움, 근접
　(= vicinity)

in close **proximity** 아주 가까이에
geographical **proximity** 지리적인 근접성

There is no bar in close proximity to my house.
집에서 아주 가까운 곳에는 술집이 없다.
Geographic proximity to the park is a vital factor.
공원으로의 지리적인 근접성은 중요한 요소이다.

Day 3 만남 Encounter 39

Unit 02 봉사단체

LET'S STUDY

enclose
[inklóuz]
동 동봉하다; 에워싸다

▶ enclosure
  명 동봉한 것; 둘러싼 곳

enclose an envelope 봉투를 동봉하다
enclose a photograph 사진을 동봉하다

We've enclosed an envelope for your convenience.
당신의 편의를 위해 봉투를 동봉했다.
I'm also enclosing a photograph of your parents.
당신 부모님의 사진 한 장도 동봉한다.

---

assign
[əsáin]
동 배정하다, 맡기다

▶ assignment
  명 임무, 과제

assign a role 역할을 배정하다
assign a value 가치를 부여하다

I'll assign a role for each person in this meeting.
나는 이 회의에서 각자가 맡을 역할을 배정할 것이다.
Assign a value to every moment of your life.
인생의 모든 순간에 가치를 부여해라.

---

charitable
[tʃǽritəbl]
형 자비로운, 자선의

▶ charity
  명 자비, 자선

a **charitable** organization 자선 기관
a **charitable** activity 자선 활동

Evan wants to work for a charitable organization.
에반은 자선 기관을 위해 일하기를 원한다.
I plan to participate in a charitable activity this summer.
나는 이번 여름에 자선 활동에 참여할 계획이다.

---

merit
[mérit]
명 장점(= advantage);
가치(= value)

an individual **merit** 각자의 장점
an artistic **merit** 예술적 가치

A book should be judged on its individual merits.
책은 그만의 장점을 기반으로 평가되어야 한다.
I can't see any artistic merits in her paintings.
나는 그녀의 그림들에서 어떤 예술적 가치도 볼 수 없다.

---

corrupt
[kərʌ́pt]
형 타락한, 부도덕한
동 타락시키다

▶ corruption
  명 부정, 부패

a **corrupt** leader 타락한 지도자
a **corrupt** politician 타락한 정치인

A corrupt leader can put a lot of people in danger.
타락한 지도자는 많은 이들을 위험에 빠뜨릴 수 있다.
The mayor has proved that he isn't a corrupt politician.
시장은 자신이 타락한 정치인이 아님을 증명했다.

Unit 03 잘생겼군요

LET'S STUDY

notable
[nóutəbl]

- 형 주목할 만한
  (= noteworthy)
- 명 유명인
  (= celebrity)

a notable feature 주목할 만한 특징
be notable for ~으로 유명하다

One notable feature of this house is its unique roof.
이 집의 주목할 만한 특징 한 가지는 특이한 지붕이다.
This bakery is notable for its fresh baguettes.
이 빵집은 신선한 바게트로 유명하다.

concede
[kənsí:d]

- 동 인정하다; 양보하다

▶ concession
  명 인정; 양보

concede defeat 패배를 인정하다
concede the point 그 점을 인정하다

I think I'm not ready to concede defeat yet.
나는 아직 패배를 인정할 준비가 안 된 것 같다.
I concede the point that smoking is bad for my health.
나는 흡연이 건강에 나쁘다는 점은 인정한다.

continual
[kəntínjuəl]

- 형 계속된

▶ continually
  부 끊임없이

continual complaints 계속된 불평
continual improvements 계속된 개선

I can't stand her continual complaints anymore.
나는 더 이상 그녀의 계속된 불평을 견딜 수가 없다.
Our company needs to make continual improvements.
우리 회사는 계속된 개선을 해나가야 한다.

conflict
[kánflikt]

- 명 분쟁(= fight)

provoke a conflict 분쟁을 야기하다
resolve a conflict 분쟁을 해결하다

Grata was the one who provoked the conflict.
그레타가 그 분쟁을 야기했던 사람이었다.
I know how to resolve conflicts between friends.
나는 친구들 사이의 분쟁을 해결하는 방법을 안다.

flaw
[flɔ:]

- 명 결점(= defect)

a fatal flaw 치명적 결점
detect a flaw 결점을 발견하다

It's her fatal flaw that she doesn't listen to others.
다른 사람들의 말을 듣지 않는 것이 그녀의 치명적 결점이다.
This program can detect flaws in your computer.
이 프로그램이 당신 컴퓨터의 결점을 발견할 수 있다.

Day 3 만남 Encounter

Unit 04

카부츠 벼룩시장의 그녀

LET'S STUDY

extent [ikstént] 명 정도, 범위(= degree)	to some **extent** 어느 정도까지 to the full **extent** 최대 한도까지 I admit that it was my fault to some extent. 어느 정도까지는 내 잘못이었음을 인정한다. He should be punished to the full extent of the law. 그는 법의 최대 한도까지 심판받아야 한다.
barter [bá:rtər] 명 물물교환 동 물물교환 하다(= swap)	a barter **system** 물물교환 시스템 a barer **agreement** 물물교환 협정 Some tribes in Africa still rely on a barter system. 아프리카의 몇몇 부족들은 아직도 물물교환에 의존한다. The two countries arranged a barter agreement. 그 두 나라는 물물교환 협정을 맺었다.
obsolete [àbsəlí:t] 형 사용되지 않는, 쓸모없는(= disused); 구식의(= outdated)	become **obsolete** 쓸모없이 되다 render A **obsolete** A를 쓸모없게 만들다 Paper books may become obsolete at school. 종이책은 학교에서 쓸모없게 될 수도 있다. CDs and MP3s rendered cassette tapes obsolete. CD와 MP3가 카세트 테이프를 쓸모없게 만들었다.
expenditure [ikspénditʃər] 명 지출(= spending)	reduce **expenditure** on ~의 지출을 줄이다 increase **expenditure** on ~의 지출을 늘리다 Gwen decided to reduce expenditure on food. 그웬은 식비를 줄이기로 결심했다. We planed to increase expenditure on marketing. 우리는 마케팅 비용을 늘리기로 계획했다.
consumption [kənsʌ́mpʃən] 명 소비; 섭취 ▶ consume 　동 소비하다 ▶ consumer 　명 소비자	energy **consumption** 에너지 소비 alcohol **consumption** 알코올 섭취 The energy consumption rises each year. 에너지 소비는 매년 증가한다. Alcohol consumption may cause high blood pressure. 알코올 섭취는 고혈압을 일으킬 수 있다.

Day 3 만남 Encounter 45

Review Test

1 다음 단어의 뜻을 고르세요.

1) continual   a. 진정한   b. 계속된

2) enclose   a. 동봉하다   b. 인정하다

3) corrupt   a. 타락한   b. 진정한

4) consumption   a. 결점   b. 소비

5) emerge   a. 나오다   b. 배정하다

2 각 문장에서 밑줄 친 부분에 해당하는 뜻을 포함한 단어를 보기에서 찾아 쓰세요.

> notable   extent   merit   vigorous   glance   expenditure

1) 영국 봉사단체는 장점을 많이 가지고 있어.   (   )

2) 한 눈에 알아보겠다!   (   )

3) 그런 애는 성격도 활발할 듯.   (   )

4) 저기 있는 남자애 주목할 만하지 않아?   (   )

5) 생활 지출을 줄이려면 여기서 쇼핑하는 것이 최고예요.   (   )

Answer Key
1. (1) b. 계속된 (2) a. 동봉하다 (3) a. 타락한 (4) b. 소비 (5) a. 나오다
2. (1) merit (2) glance (3) vigorous (4) notable (5) expenditure

3 각 단어를 유의어와 연결하세요.

1) conflict • • a. defect

2) obsolete • • b. swap

3) flaw • • c. fight

4) genuine • • d. real

5) barter • • e. disused

4 각 문장의 빈칸에 가장 알맞은 단어를 보기에서 찾아 쓰세요.

> proximity concede charitable extent glance assign

1) I admit that it was my fault to some _____.

2) Evan wants to work for a(an) _____ organization.

3) I think I'm not ready to _____ defeat yet.

4) I'll _____ a role for each person in this meeting.

5) There is no bar in close _____ to my house.

Answer Key

3. (1) c. fight (2) e. disused (3) a. defect (4) d. real (5) b. swap
4. (1) extent (2) charitable (3) concede (4) assign (5) proximity

Let's Speak

Unit 1

Student A Did you see the girl emerging from the teachers' room?
Student B She's a genuine beauty! A girl like her must have a vigorous personality.
Monica Is the seat taken?
Allie No, have a seat. (Oh, this must be the girl. I can recognize her at a glance. I can't believe she is sitting at this close proximity.)
Allie Hi! It's Allie.
Monica I'm Monica.

Unit 2

Allie Even though I'm in England, I don't have any chance to make English friends.
Monica How about sending a mail enclosing a certain application to a volunteer organization? Then they will assign someone for you.
Allie There are many charitable people here.
Monica The organizations here have many merits, and they rarely have a corrupt image.

Unit 3

Allie Monica! That guy over there is really notable, isn't he?
Monica Ah, him! He's my ex-boyfriend.
Allie Really?
Monica I have to concede that he's quite good looking. But, he has a really bad character. His continual self-flattering always leads to a conflict with others.
Allie That's a fatal flaw.

Unit 4

Allie Can you give me a discount on this heater?
Carol I can do it for you to some extent. Or you can barter with other things you have. By the way, this is almost spring time. Wouldn't a heater be obsolete?
Allie The houses here are really cold.
Carol Oh, you came here to study. This is the best place for shopping if you plan to reduce your expenditure. This is really smart consumption.

Day 4

쇼핑 Shopping

Preview

- cooperate
- committee
- display
- souvenir
- smuggle
- acid
- emit
- contaminate
- erode
- eliminate
- wholesale
- assemble
- dimension
- reasonable
- durable
- stain
- operate
- quality
- stock
- voluntary

Unit 01 차이나타운

LET'S STUDY

cooperate
[kouápərèit]
⑤ 협동하다, 협력하다

▶ cooperation
  ⑲ 협동
▶ cooperative
  ⑲ 협동적인

cooperate with ~와 협동하다
cooperate in ~에 대해 협력하다

We have to cooperate with each other to survive.
우리는 살아남기 위해서 서로 협동해야만 한다.
Lily and Maria cooperated in making the new recipe.
릴리와 마리아는 그 새로운 요리법 개발에 협력했다.

committee
[kəmíti]
⑲ 위원회
  (= commission)

an advisory **committee** 자문 위원회
an executive **committee** 집행 위원회

I'm a member of the Education Advisory Committee.
나는 교육 자문 위원회의 회원이다.
There will be an executive committee meeting soon.
곧 집행 위원회 회의가 있을 것이다.

display
[displéi]
⑤ 진열하다(= array),
  전시하다(= exhibit)
⑲ 진열, 전시

display an object 물건을 진열하다
display knowledge 지식을 드러내다

I want to display beautiful objects on the top shelf.
나는 맨 위의 선반에는 아름다운 물건들을 진열하고 싶다.
Audrey displayed her knowledge of literature.
오드리는 문학작품에 대한 그녀의 지식을 드러냈다.

souvenir
[sùːvəníər]
⑲ 기념품(= memento)

a **souvenir** shop 기념품 가게
a **souvenir** postcard 기념 엽서

There is a souvenir shop next to the exit.
출구 옆에 기념품 가게가 있다.
Susan bought a collection of souvenir postcards.
수잔은 기념 엽서 모음집을 샀다.

smuggle
[smʌ́gl]
⑤ 밀수하다

▶ smuggler
  ⑲ 밀수입자

be **smuggled** out of ~에서 밀반출되다
be **smuggled** into ~으로 밀수입되다

Many illegal drugs have been smuggled out of China.
많은 불법 약들이 중국에서 밀반출되어 왔다.
The stolen diamond was smuggled into France.
그 도난당한 다이아몬드는 프랑스로 밀수입되었다.

Unit 02 우산은 필수

LET'S STUDY

acid
[ǽsid]
- 명 산성(= acidity)
- 형 산성의(= acidic)

acid rain 산성비
acid soil 산성 토양

Acid rain can cause damage to animals and plants.
산성비는 동식물들에게 해를 끼칠 수 있다.
Some plants can grow well in acid soil.
어떤 식물들은 산성 토양에서 잘 자랄 수 있다.

---

emit
[imít]
- 동 배출하다
- ▶ emission
  명 배출

emit pollutants 오염 물질을 배출하다
emit electromagnetic waves 전자파를 방출하다

Cars emit pollutants that cause air pollution.
차는 공기 오염을 일으키는 오염 물질을 배출한다.
Most home appliances emit electromagnetic waves.
대부분의 가정용 전기기기들은 전자파를 방출한다.

---

contaminate
[kəntǽmənit]
- 동 오염시키다; 악영향을 주다
- ▶ contamination
  명 오염; 감염

contaminate the water 물을 오염시키다
contaminate the air 공기를 오염시키다

The toxins from the factory contaminated the water.
그 공장에서 나온 독소들이 물을 오염시켰다.
Radioactivity can contaminate the air seriously.
방사능은 공기를 심각하게 오염시킬 수 있다.

---

erode
[iróud]
- 동 부식시키다, 침식시키다; 약하게 하다
- ▶ erosion
  명 부식, 침식

erode a rock 바위를 침식시키다
erode a relationship 관계를 무너뜨리다

The waves have eroded the rocks on the beach.
파도가 해변의 바위들을 침식시켰다.
A careless word can easily erode a relationship.
부주의한 말은 쉽게 관계를 무너뜨릴 수 있다.

---

eliminate
[ilímənèit]
- 동 제거하다, 없애다 (= remove)
- ▶ elimination
  명 제거

eliminate a problem 문제를 제거하다
eliminate the need 필요성을 없애다

We have eliminated the problems we were facing.
우리는 우리에게 닥친 문제들을 제거했다.
Smart phones eliminated the need for a camera.
스마트폰은 카메라의 필요성을 없앴다.

Day 4 쇼핑 Shopping

LET'S STUDY

wholesale
[hóulsèil]

- 혱 도매의
  (↔ 소매의 retail)
- 명 도매
- 부 도매로

a **wholesale** price 도매가
a **wholesale** market 도매시장

The wholesale price of this bag will increase soon.
이 가방의 도매가가 곧 오를 것이다.
You can buy it at half price in a wholesale market.
당신은 이것을 도매시장에서 반값에 살 수 있다.

assemble
[əsémbl]

- 동 조립하다
  (= construct);
  모으다(= amass)

assemble parts 부품을 조립하다
assemble a team 팀을 만들다

I need help to assemble the parts of this table.
내가 이 테이블의 부품들을 조립하는 데 도움이 필요하다.
It took me two months to assemble my own team.
내 팀을 만드는 데 두 달이 걸렸다.

dimension
[dimén ʃən]

- 명 치수, 크기(= size);
  관점, 측면(= view)

dimensions of a room 방의 크기
a new **dimension** 새로운 면

The decorator measured the dimensions of the room.
그 실내 장식가가 그 방의 크기를 쟀다.
Our baby added a new dimension to our marriage.
아이는 우리의 결혼 생활에 새로운 면을 더했다.

reasonable
[ríːzənəbl]

- 형 합리적인(= fair)

a **reasonable** price 합리적인 가격
a **reasonable** excuse 타당한 이유

This new car is now available at a reasonable price.
이 새차는 지금 합리적인 가격에 구입이 가능하다.
I have a reasonable excuse for being late.
나는 지각한 것에 대한 타당한 이유가 있다.

durable
[djú(ː)ərəbl]

- 형 튼튼한, 견고한

▶ durability
  명 내구성

a **durable** material 튼튼한 재료
a **durable** peace 견고한 평화

This house was built with the most durable materials.
이 집은 가장 튼튼한 재료로 지어졌다.
We will build a durable peace without a war.
우리는 전쟁 없이 견고한 평화를 이뤄낼 것이다.

Unit 04 자선가게에서 쇼핑

LET'S STUDY

stain [stein] 명 얼룩, 자국(= spot) 동 더럽히다(= defile)	a wine **stain** 와인 얼룩 a blood **stain** 핏자국 It's hard to remove a wine stain from a white dress. 하얀 드레스에서 와인 얼룩을 제거하기 힘들다. The blood stain on the floor is evidence of the accident. 바닥의 핏자국이 그 사고의 증거이다.
operate [ápərèit] 동 운영하다; 작동하다; 수술하다 ▶ operation 명 운영; 수술	**operate** a business 사업을 운영하다 **operate** a machine 기계를 작동하다 Martin operates a business with his friends. 마틴은 친구들과 함께 사업을 운영한다. Only trained technicians can operate this machine. 훈련받은 기술자들만이 이 기계를 작동할 수 있다.
quality [kwάləti] 명 품질; 성질 형 양질의(= prime)	maintain **quality** 품질을 유지하다 improve **quality** 품질을 향상시키다 We will maintain the quality of service at all times. 우리는 언제나 서비스의 질을 유지할 것이다. Good books can improve the quality of life. 좋은 책은 삶의 질을 높여줄 수 있다.
stock [stɑk] 명 재고(= inventory); 주식 형 재고가 있는 동 제공하다	in **stock** 재고가 있는 **stock** market 주식 시장 I am sorry that we don't have your size in stock. 죄송하지만 당신의 사이즈는 재고가 없습니다. June can be a very good time for the stock market. 6월은 주식 시장에 아주 좋은 때가 될 수도 있다.
voluntary [vάləntèri] 형 자발적인 명 자발적인 행동 ▶ voluntarily 부 자발적으로	**voluntary** work 자원 봉사 a **voluntary** effort 자발적인 노력 I think Eva spends too much time on voluntary work. 나는 에바가 자원 봉사에 너무 많은 시간을 쓰는 것 같다. We have to increase voluntary efforts to reduce waste. 우리는 쓰레기를 줄이기 위해 자발적인 노력을 더 해야 한다.

Review Test

1 다음 단어의 뜻을 고르세요.

1) erode   a. 부식시키다   b. 제거하다

2) smuggle   a. 전시하다   b. 밀수하다

3) committee   a. 재고   b. 위원회

4) wholesale   a. 도매의   b. 견고한

5) voluntary   a. 합리적인   b. 자발적인

2 각 문장에서 밑줄 친 부분에 해당하는 뜻을 포함한 단어를 보기에서 찾아 쓰세요.

> emit   operate   quality   display   assemble   acid

1) 봉사단체들이 운영하는 곳이야.   (　　　　)

2) 산성비가 아니라서 다행인 줄 알아.   (　　　　)

3) 네가 조립해야 하는데 괜찮겠어?   (　　　　)

4) 품질 좋은 중고들만 취급해.   (　　　　)

5) 한때는 공장에서 오염 물질을 많이 배출했어.   (　　　　)

Answer Key

1. (1) a. 부식시키다 (2) b. 밀수하다 (3) b. 위원회 (4) a. 도매의 (5) b. 자발적인
2. (1) operate (2) acid (3) assemble (4) quality (5) emit

3 각 단어를 유의어와 연결하세요.

1) dimension •   • a. fair

2) eliminate •   • b. memento

3) souvenir •   • c. spot

4) reasonable •   • d. size

5) stain •   • e. remove

4 각 문장의 빈칸에 가장 알맞은 단어를 보기에서 찾아 쓰세요.

> durable   stock   contaminate   quality   display   cooperate

1) We have to _____ with each other to survive.

2) Radioactivity can _____ the air seriously.

3) This house was built with the most _____ materials.

4) I want to _____ beautiful objects on the top shelf.

5) I am sorry that we don't have your size in _____.

Answer Key

3. (1) d. size (2) e. remove (3) b. memento (4) a. fair (5) c. spot
4. (1) cooperate (2) contaminate (3) durable (4) display (5) stock

Let's Speak

Unit 1

Allie   Chinese people cooperate wherever they go.
Yang   We also have our own committee here.
Allie   Look at the souvenirs displayed in this store! Do you think there are any smuggled goods deep inside the store?
Yang   Not sure. Rumors say that you can get anything existing in the world in Chinatown.

Unit 2

Carol   How can you not bring an umbrella when coming to England? It's good for you that it's not acid rain anymore. In the past, many factories used to emit a lot of pollutants. So the acid rain contaminated the water in the Thames, and even eroded the outside of Westminster Abbey. With a lot of efforts, we almost eliminated the pollutants.

Unit 3

Yang   The products here are almost as low as the wholesale price. Instead, you have to assemble them by yourself. Would that be okay?
Allie   I'll buy you dinner, and you will help me.
This seems to be adequate considering the dimension of my room. It also looks durable enough for this reasonable price.
Yang   Try to be quick.

Unit 4

Monica   I bought a Dior scarf at 5 pounds in this store. Although it had a small stain, it was a great deal.
Allie   What kind of shop is it?
Monica   Don't you know? Volunteer organizations operate these shops, and they're everywhere. They sell high-quality used goods, and those goods are the only ones in stock. You can pick up a valuable item if you are lucky. My ex-boyfriend once did voluntary work there.

Day 5

건강 Health

Preview

- trivial
- terminal
- contagious
- ominous
- prescribe
- undergo
- costly
- dispose
- vanish
- evident
- nutrition
- chronic
- susceptible
- surplus
- renewal
- accumulate
- antiseptic
- extract
- soothe
- fragrant

Unit 01 전염되나요

LET'S STUDY

trivial
[tríviəl]
- 형 사소한 (= petty)

a **trivial** issue 사소한 문제
a **trivial** reason 사소한 이유

We've been arguing over a trivial issue for hours.
우리는 사소한 문제에 대해 몇 시간째 논쟁하고 있다.
People often commit a crime for trivial reasons.
사람들은 종종 사소한 이유로 범죄를 저지른다.

terminal
[tə́ːrmənəl]
- 형 불치의; 말기의
- 명 종점

▶ terminate
  동 끝내다, 종료하다

a **terminal** illness 불치병
terminal cancer 말기암

Henry was diagnosed with a terminal illness.
헨리는 불치병을 진단받았다.
My sister is suffering from terminal cancer.
내 여동생은 말기암을 앓고 있다.

contagious
[kəntéidʒəs]
- 형 전염성 있는
  (= infectious)

a **contagious** disease 전염성 질병
highly **contagious** 전염성이 높은

Olivia didn't know she had a contagious disease.
올리비아는 그녀가 전염성 질병에 걸렸는지 몰랐다.
This virus is said to be highly contagious.
이 바이러스는 전염성이 높다고 알려져 있다.

ominous
[ámənəs]
- 형 불길한

▶ omen
  명 불길한 예감
▶ ominously
  부 불길하게

an **ominous** sign 불길한 징조
an **ominous** silence 불길한 침묵

The broken mirror is an ominous sign for our plan.
그 깨진 거울은 우리의 계획에 대한 불길한 징조이다.
A short, but ominous silence followed the speech.
그 연설 후에 짧지만 불길한 침묵이 뒤따랐다.

prescribe
[priskráib]
- 동 처방하다

▶ prescription
  명 처방전

prescribe medicine 약을 처방하다
prescribe an antibiotic 항생제를 처방하다

The doctor prescribed medicine to relieve my pain.
의사는 내 고통을 완화시키기 위해 약을 처방했다.
I try not to prescribe antibiotics to patients if possible.
나는 가능한 한 환자들에게 항생제를 처방하지 않으려고 한다.

Unit 02 환경이 안 좋아

LET'S STUDY

undergo
[ʌ̀ndərgóu]
동 받다, 겪다
(= go through)

undergo a medical examination 건강검진을 받다
undergo a change 변화를 겪다

I need to undergo a medical examination every year.
나는 매년 건강검진을 받아야 한다.
Our company is undergoing a significant change.
우리 회사는 중요한 변화를 겪고 있는 중이다.

costly
[kɔ́(:)stli]
형 값비싼(= pricy)

a costly penalty 값비싼 벌금
a costly mistake 큰 실수

You will have to pay a costly penalty for this.
당신은 이것 때문에 값비싼 벌금을 내야 할 것이다.
Cindy was fired after making a costly mistake.
신디는 큰 실수를 한 후 해고당했다.

dispose
[dispóuz]
동 처분하다; 배치하다

▶ disposal
명 처리, 처분
▶ disposition
명 배치, 성향

dispose of waste 쓰레기를 버리다
dispose of a body 시체를 유기하다

The factory disposed of toxic waste in the river.
그 공장은 유독성 폐기물을 강에 버렸다.
I know where the murderer disposed of Jane's body.
나는 그 살인자가 어디에 제인의 시체를 유기했는지 안다.

vanish
[vǽniʃ]
동 사라지다
(= disappear)

vanish from ~에서 사라지다
vanish into ~속으로 사라지다

The actress suddenly vanished from the stage.
그 여배우는 갑자기 무대에서 사라졌다.
I was watching him vanishing into the darkness.
나는 그가 어둠속으로 사라지는 것을 보고 있었다.

evident
[évidənt]
형 분명한, 뚜렷한
(= distinct)

evident pride 분명한 자신감
evident delight 뚜렷한 기쁨

Jack explained his project with evident pride.
잭은 분명한 자신감을 가지고 그의 프로젝트를 설명했다.
Maria accepted the necklace with evident delight.
마리아는 뚜렷한 기쁨을 보이며 목걸이를 받았다.

Unit 03 영양 결핍

LET'S STUDY

nutrition
[nju:tríʃən]
명 영양, 영양 섭취

▶ nutritious
형 영양분이 있는

poor nutrition 영양 부족
proper nutrition 적절한 영양 섭취

Poor nutrition can cause a lot of health problems.
영양 부족은 많은 건강 문제를 야기할 수 있다.
I want to learn about proper nutrition for my family.
우리 가족을 위해 적절한 영양 섭취에 대해 배우고 싶다.

chronic
[kránik]
형 만성의(= inveterate)

chronic indigestion 만성 소화불량
chronic anxiety 만성 불안

I've been suffering from chronic indigestion for years.
나는 오랫동안 만성 소화불량을 앓고 있다.
Chronic anxiety might lead to severe depression.
만성 불안은 심각한 우울증으로 이어질 수 있다.

susceptible
[səséptəbl]
형 감염되기 쉬운; 민감한

▶ susceptibility
명 민감성

susceptible to disease 질병에 걸리기 쉬운
susceptible to injury 부상을 당하기 쉬운

The HIV virus makes your body susceptible to disease.
에이즈 바이러스는 몸이 질병에 걸리기 쉽게 만든다.
Lack of exercise made my body susceptible to injury.
운동 부족 때문에 내 몸이 부상을 당하기 쉽게 되었다.

surplus
[sə́:rplʌs]
형 과잉의(= excess)
명 여분(= spare)

surplus fat 과잉 지방
surplus cash 여분의 돈

The best way of losing surplus fat is regular exercise.
과잉 지방을 없애는 가장 좋은 방법은 꾸준한 운동이다.
I want to invest my surplus cash in your company.
나는 여분의 돈을 네 회사에 투자하고 싶다.

renewal
[rinjú:əl]
명 갱신; 회복

▶ renew
동 갱신시키다; 회복시키다

membership renewal 멤버십 갱신
renewal date 갱신 날짜

We have an automatic membership renewal system.
우리는 자동 멤버십 갱신 시스템을 가지고 있다.
We will call you again before your renewal date.
갱신 날짜 전에 다시 전화 드리겠습니다.

Unit 04 왕여드름을 달고

LET'S STUDY

accumulate [əkjúːmjulèit] 동 쌓다, 축적하다 ▶ accumulation 명 축적	**accumulate** stress 스트레스를 쌓다 **accumulate** wealth 부를 축적하다 I've been accumulating stress while working here. 나는 여기서 일하면서 스트레스를 쌓아왔다. Leo has accumulated great wealth in an honest way. 레오는 정직한 방법으로 엄청난 부를 축적했다.
antiseptic [æntiséptik] 명 소독약; 방부제 형 소독된(= germfree)	**antiseptic** cream 소독 크림 an **antiseptic** smell 소독약 냄새 Jenny applied some antiseptic cream to my cut. 제니가 내 상처에 소독 크림을 발라주었다. I hate going to the hospital due to its antiseptic smell. 나는 소독약 냄새 때문에 병원에 가는 것을 싫어한다.
extract [ékstrækt] 동 추출하다 명 추출물 ▶ extraction 명 추출	**extract** oil 오일을 추출하다 **extract** information 정보를 뽑아내다 Clara knows how to extract essential oil from a rose. 클라라는 장미에서 에센셜 오일을 추출하는 법을 안다. It's your job to extract information from the secretary. 그 비서에게서 정보를 뽑아내는 것이 너의 임무이다.
soothe [suːð] 동 진정시키다(= alleviate); 위로하다(= console)	**soothe** a skin 피부를 진정시키다 **soothe** nerves 마음을 진정시키다 Sliced cucumbers will help soothe your skin. 얇게 썬 오이가 피부를 진정시키는데 도움을 줄 것이다. I think a cup of tea can soothe your nerves. 한 잔의 차가 네 마음을 진정시킬 수 있을 것 같다.
fragrant [fréigrənt] 형 향기로운 ▶ fragrance 명 향기	a **fragrant** flower 향기로운 꽃 a **fragrant** wine 향기로운 와인 This room is filled with fragrant flowers. 이 방은 향기로운 꽃으로 가득 찼다. A fragrant wine is essential for a romantic dinner. 로맨틱한 저녁식사에 향기로운 와인은 필수적이다.

Review Test

1 다음 단어의 뜻을 고르세요.

1) extract   a. 받다   b. 추출하다

2) fragrant   a. 과잉의   b. 향기로운

3) antiseptic   a. 소독약   b. 갱신

4) ominous   a. 불길한   b. 사소한

5) prescribe   a. 사라지다   b. 처방하다

2 각 문장에서 밑줄 친 부분에 해당하는 뜻을 포함한 단어를 보기에서 찾아 쓰세요.

> dispose   evident   undergo   accumulate   chronic   terminal

1) 스트레스를 너무 <u>쌓아뒀나</u> 봐.   (   )

2) <u>불치병</u>이면 어떡해요?   (   )

3) 정말 빈대 때문이었던 게 <u>분명하네</u>.   (   )

4) <u>만성</u> 소화불량일지도 몰라.   (   )

5) 일단 침대부터 <u>처분해</u> 보는 걸 추천해.   (   )

Answer Key
1. (1) b. 추출하다 (2) b. 향기로운 (3) a. 소독약 (4) a. 불길한 (5) b. 처방하다
2. (1) accumulate (2) terminal (3) evident (4) chronic (5) dispose

3 각 단어를 유의어와 연결하세요.

1) surplus   •   • a. petty

2) trivial   •   • b. disappear

3) soothe   •   • c. pricy

4) costly   •   • d. excess

5) vanish   •   • e. alleviate

4 각 문장의 빈칸에 가장 알맞은 단어를 보기에서 찾아 쓰세요.

> renewal susceptible contagious nutrition evident undergo

1) The HIV virus makes your body _____ to disease.

2) I need to _____ a medical examination every year.

3) Poor _____ can cause a lot of health problems.

4) We have an automatic membership _____ system.

5) Olivia didn't know she had a(an) _____ disease.

Answer Key
3. (1) d. excess (2) a. petty (3) e. alleviate (4) c. pricy (5) b. disappear
4. (1) susceptible (2) undergo (3) nutrition (4) renewal (5) contagious

Let's Speak

Unit 1

Allie What's this spot? Probably just something trivial. (I feel like it's getting worse, but that's probably just my imagination. Why am I getting more and more spots?) What should I do if this is a terminal illness? If it is something contagious, will I get deported? I have really ominous feelings.

Doctor I will prescribe you some allergy medicines for now. Let's wait and see what happens.

Unit 2

Yang Didn't you say that you are taking medicine? Why aren't you getting better?

Allie I have no idea. I guess I should undergo a medical examination. I heard that it's quite costly.

Yang Maybe it's just because of bedbugs, you know?

Allie No way! Who has bedbugs these days?

Yang You know that the furniture in our flat is somewhat old and shabby. I heard that one of the tenants in our house had a similar problem last year. I recommend that you dispose of your bed first.

Allie All the spots have vanished. It's evident that they were from bed bugs.

Unit 3

Allie *I've been eating only ramen because cooking is too much work. I think my body lacks proper nutrition.* I feel bloated all the time. I might be suffering from chronic indigestion.

Monica You should have a square meal. If your health fails, your body will become susceptible to disease. I'm also worried about the surplus fat in my body. My gym membership is up for renewal.

Unit 4

Monica What's that on your cheek?

Allie I guess I've been accumulating a lot of stress. I found it this morning.

Monica You should have applied antiseptic on it.
Let's drop by a drug store on the way. The essence extracted from bee venom works well. It will soothe your skin.

Allie I only use fragrant cosmetics though.

Monica This is not the time to care about it.

Day 6

일상 Daily Life

Preview

- ☐ sophisticated
- ☐ exorbitant
- ☐ erroneous
- ☐ customary
- ☐ comply
- ☐ shrink
- ☐ charge
- ☐ effective
- ☐ appeal
- ☐ manipulate
- ☐ pastime
- ☐ versatile
- ☐ compliment
- ☐ modest
- ☐ awkward
- ☐ temporary
- ☐ overseas
- ☐ substantial
- ☐ negotiate
- ☐ enthusiasm

Unit 01 초여름의 꿈

LET'S STUDY

sophisticated
[səfístəkèitid]
형 교양 있는
(= cultivated)

a **sophisticated** woman 교양 있는 여자
a **sophisticated** manner 예의 바른 태도

Roxy is such a beautiful and sophisticated woman.
록시는 정말 아름답고 교양 있는 여자이다.
Noah escorted me to dinner in a sophisticated manner.
노아는 예의 바른 태도로 저녁식사에 나를 에스코트했다.

---

exorbitant
[igzɔ́ːrbitənt]
형 과도한(= inordinate), 터무니없는
(= outrageous)

an **exorbitant** charge 과도한 요금
an **exorbitant** interest rate 과도한 이자율

Peter paid an exorbitant charge to rent a car.
피터는 차를 대여하기 위해 과도한 요금을 지불했다.
The bank is notorious for its exorbitant interest rate.
그 은행은 과도한 이자율로 악명이 높다.

---

erroneous
[iróuniəs]
형 잘못된

▶ erroneously
부 잘못되게

an **erroneous** assumption 잘못된 추측
an **erroneous** conclusion 잘못된 결론

I think you made an erroneous assumption about her.
내 생각에 네가 그녀에 대해 잘못된 추측을 했던 것 같다.
The police came to an erroneous conclusion.
경찰은 잘못된 결론을 내렸다.

---

customary
[kʌ́stəmèri]
형 관례적인, 관습적인

▶ custom
명 관습

customary attire 관례적 의복
a **customary** practice 관행

The customary wedding attire for men is a tuxedo.
남자들의 관례적인 결혼 의복은 턱시도이다.
It's a customary practice to send an e-mail first.
이메일을 먼저 보내는 것이 관행이다.

---

comply
[kəmplái]
동 따르다, 동의하다

▶ compliance
명 따름, 순종

comply with a duty 의무를 따르다
comply with a demand 요구를 따르다

I will comply with my duties as a citizen.
나는 시민으로서 나의 의무를 따를 것이다.
We have to comply with their demands for this once.
우리는 이번만은 그들의 요구를 따라야 한다.

Day 6 일상 Daily Life

Unit 02 픽업아티스트

LET'S STUDY

shrink
[ʃriŋk]
동 줄어들다, 줄다
(= decrease)

shrink back 움츠러들다
shrink to ~으로 줄어들다

The thief shrank back when he saw a policeman.
그 도둑은 경찰을 보고 움츠러들었다.
The population of our town has shrunk to 200 people.
우리 마을의 인구가 200명으로 줄어들었다.

charge
[tʃɑːrdʒ]
동 비용을 청구하다(= bill)
명 비용

charge a rent 집세를 청구하다
charge an interest rate 이자를 청구하다

The landlord charges no rent for the room upstairs.
집주인은 위층의 그 방에는 집세를 청구하지 않는다.
The mortgage company charges a high interest rate.
그 주택 융자 회사는 높은 이자를 청구한다.

effective
[iféktiv]
형 효과적인
(= efficacious)

an **effective** method 효과적인 방법
an **effective** approach 효과적인 접근법

Yoga is an effective method of relieving your stress.
요가는 스트레스를 해소하는 효과적인 방법이다.
I proposed an effective approach to cancer treatment.
나는 암 치료에 효과적인 접근법을 제안했다.

appeal
[əpíːl]
동 관심을 끌다(= attract); 호소하다
명 매력

appeal to ~의 관심을 끌다
appeal for ~을 호소하다

I think this color will appeal to women in their 30s.
내 생각에 이 색깔이 30대 여성들의 관심을 끌 것 같다.
The storm victims appealed for food and shelter.
태풍 피해자들은 음식과 피난처 제공을 호소했다.

manipulate
[mənípjulèit]
동 조종하다, 조작하다

▶ manipulation
명 조종, 조작

manipulate people 사람을 조종하다
manipulate data 자료를 조작하다

Henry uses money to manipulate other people.
헨리는 다른 사람들을 조종하기 위해 돈을 사용한다.
Jane manipulated the data to get the result she wanted.
제인은 원하는 결과를 얻기 위해 자료를 조작했다.

Unit 03 운명의 장난

LET'S STUDY

pastime
[pǽstàim]
명 취미(= hobby), 놀이

a national pastime 국민적 오락
a popular pastime 인기 있는 놀이

Football is a national pastime of the United States.
미식축구는 미국의 국민적 오락이다.
Playing online games is a popular pastime.
온라인 게임은 인기 있는 놀이이다.

---

versatile
[və́ːrsətil]
형 다재다능한

▶ versatility
명 다재다능

a versatile genius 다재다능한 천재
a versatile tool 다용도의 도구

We all think that Julia is a versatile genius.
우리 모두는 줄리아가 다재다능한 천재라고 생각한다.
This versatile tool can be used for different purposes.
이 다용도의 도구는 여러 가지 목적으로 사용될 수 있다.

---

compliment
[kámpləmənt]
명 칭찬(= praise)

pay a compliment 칭찬을 하다
accept a compliment 칭찬을 받아들이다

I paid a compliment to my students for their hard work.
나는 학생들이 열심히 공부한 것에 대해 칭찬을 했다.
I'll gladly accept your compliment.
당신의 칭찬을 기쁘게 받아들이겠다.

---

modest
[mádist]
형 겸손한(= humble);
적당한(= moderate)

a modest person 겸손한 사람
a modest demand 적당한 요구

Greta is a very modest and religious person.
그레타는 매우 겸손하고 경건한 사람이다.
It's a modest demand compared to the previous one.
이전의 요구에 비하면 적당한 요구이다.

---

awkward
[ɔ́ːkwərd]
형 어색한(= uneasy);
곤란한(= difficult)

an awkward silence 어색한 침묵
an awkward situation 곤란한 상황

There was an awkward silence as John left the room.
존이 방을 떠났을 때 어색한 침묵이 흘렀다.
Mary put me in an awkward situation at the party.
메리는 그 파티에서 나를 곤란한 상황에 빠뜨렸다.

Unit 04 희망찬 해외취업

LET'S STUDY

temporary
[témpərèri]
형 임시의

temporary residence 임시 거주
a **temporary** worker 임시 직원

Lisa is taking up a temporary residence in this hotel.
리사는 이 호텔에 임시로 거주하고 있다.
We will not hire any more temporary workers.
우리는 더 이상 임시 직원들을 고용하지 않을 것이다.

overseas
[óuvərsì:z]
부 해외에서, 해외로(= abroad)
형 해외의

travel **overseas** 해외를 여행하다
move **overseas** 해외로 이전하다

When I travel overseas, I never use a credit card.
해외를 여행할 때, 나는 절대 신용카드를 사용하지 않는다.
Many factories in our country have moved overseas.
우리나라의 많은 공장들이 해외로 이전했다.

substantial
[səbstǽnʃəl]
형 많은(= affluent); 실질적인(= real)

a **substantial** salary 많은 연봉
a **substantial** evidence 실질적인 증거

The new company offered me a substantial salary.
새로운 회사는 나에게 많은 연봉을 제시했다.
There's no substantial evidence to arrest him.
그를 체포할 만한 실질적인 증거가 없다.

negotiate
[nigóuʃièit]
동 협상하다, 협정하다
▶ negotiation
명 협상

negotiate discounts 가격 할인을 협상하다
negotiate peace 평화 협정을 하다

Sofia is good at negotiating discounts in the market.
소피아는 시장에서 가격 할인 협상에 능하다.
Our representative will negotiate peace with them.
우리의 대표가 그들과 평화 협정을 할 것이다.

enthusiasm
[inθjú:ziæ̀zəm]
명 열정, 열광
▶ enthusiastic
형 열정적인, 열광적인

enthusiasm for work 일에 대한 열정
enthusiasm for life 인생에 대한 열정

Jack seems to lack enthusiasm for his work.
잭은 일에 대한 열정이 부족한 것처럼 보인다.
I've always admired your enthusiasm for life.
나는 너의 삶에 대한 열정에 항상 감탄해왔다.

Review Test

1 다음 단어의 뜻을 고르세요.

1) shrink   a. 줄어들다   b. 따르다

2) enthusiasm   a. 취미   b. 열정

3) customary   a. 효과적인   b. 관례적인

4) negotiate   a. 관심을 끌다   b. 협상하다

5) awkward   a. 어색한   b. 과도한

2 각 문장에서 밑줄 친 부분에 해당하는 뜻을 포함한 단어를 보기에서 찾아 쓰세요.

> compliment   manipulate   comply   temporary   charge   sophisticated

1) 이 집에서 임시 거주하게 됐어요. (   )

2) 3일 과정에 500파운드나 비용을 청구한다고? (   )

3) 아, 칭찬 고마워. (   )

4) 교양 있는 여자가 된 기분이야. (   )

5) 사람 마음을 조종하려 하다니 난 정말 별로야. (   )

Answer Key
1. (1) a. 줄어들다 (2) b. 열정 (3) b. 관례적인 (4) b. 협상하다 (5) a. 어색한
2. (1) temporary (2) charge (3) compliment (4) sophisticated (5) manipulate

3 각 단어를 유의어와 연결하세요.

1) appeal   •   •   a. hobby

2) modest   •   •   b. inordinate

3) exorbitant   •   •   c. attract

4) pastime   •   •   d. abroad

5) overseas   •   •   e. humble

4 각 문장의 빈칸에 가장 알맞은 단어를 보기에서 찾아 쓰세요.

> comply   erroneous   versatile   effective   substantial   appeal

1) We all think that Julia is a(an) _____ genius.

2) The new company offered me a(an) _____ salary.

3) I will _____ with my duties as a citizen.

4) The police came to a(an) _____ conclusion.

5) Yoga is a(an) _____ method of relieving your stress.

Answer Key

3. (1) c. attract (2) e. humble (3) b. inordinate (4) a. hobby (5) d. abroad
4. (1) versatile (2) substantial (3) comply (4) erroneous (5) effective

Let's Speak

Unit 1

Allie (Sipping a cup of black tea in Kensington park, I feel like I am a very sophisticated woman. By the way, why is the charge on the bill so exorbitant?) Isn't this fee here erroneous?

Monica No, it's because a service charge is included here. This is customary here. Didn't you know?

Allie The service charge is separate, and so is the tip. I have no choice but to comply with the custom.

Unit 2

Allie This is a course for the guys who shrink back in front of women. They charge 500 pounds for a three-day course? Would it be effective enough to be worth the money?

Monica The course offers a man-to-man training on how to appeal to women. But it doesn't sound nice to manipulate other people's minds with skills. There was a time when I was hit on by a guy in London Central. But he was one of the students. I felt so embarrassed!

Unit 3

Allie (The violin and art supplies? What kind of person is he?) Excuse me. Do you do that as a pastime? You are really versatile.

Boy Thank you for the compliment!

Allie (Such a modest person, and I really enjoy talking with him. I might have a crush on him.)

Allie By the way, I'm 24 years old. How about you?

Boy Really? I'm 12 years old. Awkward…

Unit 4

Yang Allie, he just moved in next door. He is also Korean.

Chef Nice to meet you. I'm taking up a temporary residence in this house. I'm excited because this is the first time that I have ever worked overseas. I will get a substantial salary, and I also negotiated with my boss to bring my family. Call me chef Jang in London!

Allie You are full of enthusiasm.

Day 7

경험 Experience

Preview

- ☐ inclement
- ☐ torrential
- ☐ forecast
- ☐ postpone
- ☐ alternative
- ☐ nocturnal
- ☐ arrest
- ☐ fine
- ☐ eradicate
- ☐ fertilizer
- ☐ enroll
- ☐ extreme
- ☐ entail
- ☐ encourage
- ☐ extraordinary
- ☐ variation
- ☐ nominate
- ☐ legislation
- ☐ hectic
- ☐ predominant

Unit 01   런던 날씨는 예측 불가

LET'S STUDY

inclement
[inklémənt]

형 험악한 (= severe)

inclement weather 험악한 날씨
an **inclement** wind 험한 바람

You can't take this route due to inclement weather.
너는 험악한 날씨 때문에 이 길로 갈 수 없다.
This house can withstand inclement winds.
이 집은 험한 바람을 견뎌낼 수 있다.

---

torrential
[tɔ(:)rénʃəl]

형 마구 쏟아지는 (= teeming)

a **torrential** rain 폭우
a **torrential** river 급류의 강

Nothing is visible in this torrential rain.
이런 폭우 속에는 아무것도 눈에 보이지 않는다.
Emma fell into a torrential river and went missing.
에마는 급류의 강에 빠져 실종되었다.

---

forecast
[fɔ́ːrkæst]

명 (일기)예보, 예측 (= outlook)
동 예측하다 (= predict)

check the **forecast** 일기예보를 확인하다
forecast the future 미래를 예측하다

We will set a wedding date after checking the forecast.
우리는 일기예보를 확인한 후, 결혼식 날짜를 정할 것이다.
Liam excels at forecasting the future of the economy.
리암은 미래 경제를 예측하는 것에 뛰어나다.

---

postpone
[poustpóun]

동 연기하다, 미루다 (= delay)

postpone a plan 계획을 연기하다
postpone happiness 행복을 연기하다

Anna postponed her plan of travelling around Europe.
애나는 유럽을 여행하는 계획을 연기했다.
We shouldn't postpone our happiness for any reason.
우리는 어떤 이유에서든 자신의 행복을 연기해서는 안 된다.

---

alternative
[ɔːltə́ːrnətiv]

명 대안
형 대체 가능한

▶ alternate
  동 대체시키다
▶ alternately
  부 교대로

the best **alternative** 최선의 대안
a viable **alternative** 실행 가능한 대안

For now, it seems to be our best alternative.
현재로서는 이것이 최선의 대안인 것 같다.
The experts are looking for a viable alternative.
전문가들이 실행 가능한 대안을 찾고 있다.

Unit 02 밤의 정원

LET'S STUDY

nocturnal
[nɑktə́ːrnəl]
- 형 야간의(= night)

a **nocturnal** view 야경
a **nocturnal** animal 야행성 동물

You can see the best nocturnal view from this bridge.
너는 이 다리에서 최고의 야경을 볼 수 있다.
Owls and bats are famous nocturnal animals.
올빼미와 박쥐는 유명한 야행성 동물이다.

---

arrest
[ərést]
- 동 체포하다
  (= apprehend)
- 명 체포

arrest a suspect 용의자를 체포하다
an **arrest** warrant 구속 영장

Charles helped the police to arrest a suspect.
찰스는 경찰이 용의자를 체포하는 것을 도왔다.
The court issued an arrest warrant for Mr. Baker.
법원은 베이커 씨에게 구속 영장을 발부했다.

---

fine
[fain]
- 명 벌금(= forfeit)
- 동 벌금을 부과하다

pay a **fine** 벌금을 내다
collect a **fine** 벌금을 거두다

Grace paid a fine for parking in a handicapped spot.
그레이스는 장애인 전용 구역에 주차한 일로 벌금을 냈다.
William is in charge of collecting fines in this area.
윌리엄은 이 지역에서 벌금을 거두는 일을 담당하고 있다.

---

eradicate
[irǽdəkèit]
- 동 제거하다, 근절하다
  (= exterminate)

eradicate weeds 잡초를 제거하다
eradicate a disease 질병을 근절하다

You need to eradicate weeds when growing crops.
작물을 기를 때는 잡초를 제거해야 한다.
Our aim is to eradicate the disease completely.
우리의 목적은 그 질병을 완전히 근절시키는 것이다.

---

fertilizer
[fə́ːrtəlàizər]
- 명 비료

▶ fertile
  형 풍부한
▶ fertilize
  동 풍부하게 하다

apply a **fertilizer** 비료를 주다
produce a **fertilizer** 비료를 생산하다

Apply fertilizers to help the growth of the plant.
그 식물의 성장을 돕기 위해 비료를 주도록 해라.
The company is producing an organic fertilizer.
그 회사는 유기 비료를 생산하고 있다.

Day 7 경험 Experience 89

Unit 03 하늘을 날고 싶어

LET'S STUDY

enroll
[inróul]

⑧ 등록하다(= register),
  입학하다(= enter)

enroll in a program 과정에 등록하다
enroll in a university 대학에 입학하다

Matthew enrolled in a photography program last week.
매튜는 지난주에 사진 과정에 등록했다.
Many applicants are trying to enroll in this university.
많은 지원자들이 이 대학에 입학하기 위해 노력하고 있다.

---

extreme
[ikstrí:m]

⑧ 극한의, 극단적인
⑨ 극단

▶ extremely
  ⑨ 극단적으로

extreme sports 익스트림(극한) 스포츠
an **extreme** example 극단적인 예

Nora is interested in extreme sports like rope-swing.
노라는 로프스윙 같은 익스트림(극한) 스포츠에 관심이 있다.
This case is an extreme example of domestic violence.
이 사건은 가정 폭력의 극단적인 예이다.

---

entail
[intéil]

⑧ 수반하다(= involve);
  요구하다(= require)

entail a risk 위험을 수반하다
entail a loss 손실이 따르다

Driving a racing car entails a considerable risk.
경주용 차를 운전하는 것은 엄청난 위험을 수반하다.
Investment in stocks can entail a loss of a lot of money.
주식 투자에는 많은 돈의 손실이 따를 수 있다.

---

encourage
[inkɔ́:ridʒ]

⑧ 격려하다(= hearten);
  권장하다(= promote)

encourage people 사람들을 격려하다
encourage use 사용을 권장하다

The experts encouraged people to walk more.
그 전문가들은 사람들이 더 많이 걷도록 격려했다.
The campaign is encouraging use of recycled products.
그 캠페인은 재활용품의 사용을 권장하고 있다.

---

extraordinary
[ikstrɔ́:rdəneri]

⑧ 특별한, 놀라운
  (= amazing)

an **extraordinary** experience 특별한 경험
an **extraordinary** skill 특별한 기술

Talking with the writer was an extraordinary experience.
그 작가와 이야기를 나눈 것은 정말 특별한 경험이었다.
Each one of them has an extraordinary skill.
그들 모두가 특별한 기술을 가지고 있다.

Unit 04 어차피 남의 인연

LET'S STUDY

variation
[vɛ̀əriéiʃən]

명 변화; 차이

▶ vary
  동 변화시키다
▶ variable
  형 변하기 쉬운 명 변수

add variation 변화를 주다
a wide variation 많은 차이

Lily made up new steps to add variation to her dance.
릴리는 춤에 변화를 주기 위해 새로운 스텝을 개발했다.
There is a wide variation in flavors of ice cream.
아이스크림의 맛에는 많은 차이가 있다.

nominate
[námənèit]

동 선정하다, 지명하다

▶ nomination
  명 지명, 추천

be nominated for ~의 후보로 선정되다
nominate a representative 대표를 지명하다

Kenny was nominated for player of the year.
케니는 올해의 선수 후보로 선정되었다.
We will nominate a new representative in this meeting.
우리는 이 회의에서 새로운 대표를 지명할 것이다.

legislation
[lèdʒisléiʃən]

명 법안(= law); 입법(= lawmaking)

pass legislation 법안을 통과시키다
propose legislation 법안을 발의하다

It's important to pass legislation lowering tuition fees.
학비를 낮추는 법안을 통과시키는 것은 중요하다.
I plan to propose legislation to increase exports.
나는 수출을 증대시킬 수 있는 법안을 발의할 계획이다.

hectic
[héktik]

형 혼잡한(= crowded); 정신 없이 바쁜 (= hustling)

a hectic place 혼잡한 장소
a hectic schedule 바쁜 일정

I'd like to avoid a hectic place during my vacation.
나는 휴가 중에는 혼잡한 장소는 피하고 싶다.
It's been a hectic schedule for the last two weeks.
지난 2주간은 정말 바쁜 일정이었다.

predominant
[pridámənənt]

형 지배적인, 두드러진

▶ predominantly
  부 우세하게, 주로

a predominant number 지배적인 수
a predominant feature 두드러진 특징

A predominant number of respondents are women.
응답자들의 지배적인 수가 여성들이다.
The predominant feature of her face is her pretty nose.
그녀의 얼굴에서 두드러진 특징은 예쁜 코이다.

Review Test

1 다음 단어의 뜻을 고르세요.

1) fertilizer   a. 법안   b. 비료

2) arrest   a. 등록하다   b. 체포하다

3) nominate   a. 선정하다   b. 제거하다

4) torrential   a. 마구 쏟아지는   b. 혼잡한

5) extraordinary   a. 극한의   b. 특별한

2 각 문장에서 밑줄 친 부분에 해당하는 뜻을 포함한 단어를 보기에서 찾아 쓰세요.

> alternative   entail   forecast   postpone   variation   nocturnal

1) 밤에 가서 야간 풍경이라도 볼래?   (　　　　)

2) 일정을 연기해서 그냥 출근하자.   (　　　　)

3) 위험을 엄청 수반하는 거 아냐?   (　　　　)

4) 다른 대안이 없으니 돈이나 벌어야지.   (　　　　)

5) 일상에 뭔가 변화가 필요해.   (　　　　)

Answer Key

1. (1) b. 비료 (2) b. 체포하다 (3) a. 선정하다 (4) a. 마구 쏟아지는 (5) b. 특별한
2. (1) nocturnal (2) postpone (3) entail (4) alternative (5) variation

3 각 단어를 유의어와 연결하세요.

1) enroll　　　•　　　　　• a. hearten

2) inclement　•　　　　　• b. exterminate

3) encourage　•　　　　　• c. law

4) legislation　•　　　　　• d. register

5) eradicate　•　　　　　• e. severe

4 각 문장의 빈칸에 가장 알맞은 단어를 보기에서 찾아 쓰세요.

> hectic　extreme　predominant　forecast　nocturnal　fine

1) Nora is interested in _____ sports like rope-swing.

2) We will set a wedding date after checking the _____.

3) I'd like to avoid a(an) _____ place during my vacation.

4) Grace paid a(an) _____ for parking in a handicapped spot.

5) A(An) _____ number of respondents are women.

Answer Key
1. (1) d. register　(2) e. severe　(3) a. hearten　(4) c. law　(5) b. exterminate
2. (1) extreme　(2) forecast　(3) hectic　(4) fine　(5) predominant

Let's Speak

Unit 1

Allie   Yang! Did you see outside? The weather is really inclement!
Yang   You're right. This is a torrential rain. We took the day off to go to the park. What can we do?
Allie   I can't believe it! We should have checked the forecast.
Yang   Let's postpone the plan and go to work.
Allie   I don't have an alternative anyway. I should probably just earn money.

Unit 2

Allie   The rain stopped as soon as we arrived at work!
Yang   How about going there at night and enjoying the nocturnal view? If we trespass, we might get arrested or have to pay a fine. So, let's just look from outside.
Allie   Those flowers are so beautiful.
Yang   The gardeners must be eradicating the weeds, and applying fertilizer.
Allie   I want to go inside.
Yang   No, you can't.

Unit 3

Yang   Can you switch shifts with me on Monday? I've enrolled in a skydiving course.
Allie   Really? That's an extreme sport! Doesn't it entail a substantial risk? I heard about a case where people collide into each other in the air and died.
Yang   You're my friend. You should be encouraging me.
Allie   Yes. That'll be an extraordinary experience.

Unit 4

Allie   I'm bored. I need to add variation to my routine life.
Carol   How about visiting a gay club? Today's DJ is said to have been nominated for a Grammy.
Allie   Oh, wouldn't they mind if normal people go there?
Carol   I don't think they would. Now the legislation for gay marriage was passed here.
Allie   What a hectic place! Male is the predominant gender here.
Carol   People say all the handsome guys in London either gather here, or are already married.

Day 8

인생 Life

Preview

- [ ] sterile
- [ ] diagnose
- [ ] artificial
- [ ] inquire
- [ ] qualification
- [ ] convert
- [ ] conservative
- [ ] pious
- [ ] violate
- [ ] refrain
- [ ] venture
- [ ] expedition
- [ ] hostage
- [ ] assassinate
- [ ] jeopardize
- [ ] stir
- [ ] edible
- [ ] adept
- [ ] asset
- [ ] perspiration

Unit 01 함께 살자

LET'S STUDY

sterile
[stéril]
혱 불임의; 살균한

▶ sterility
혱 불임
▶ sterilize
통 불임이 되게 하다

a **sterile** couple 불임 부부
sterile water 살균한 물

The news gave new hope to many sterile couples.
그 뉴스는 많은 불임 부부에게 새로운 희망을 주었다.
It's safe to drink sterile water while travelling.
여행 중에는 살균한 물을 마시는 것이 안전하다.

---

diagnose
[dáiəgnòus]
통 진단하다

▶ diagnosis
혱 진단

diagnose a illness 병명을 진단하다
diagnose depression 우울증을 진단하다

Dr. Norman was not able to diagnose my illness.
노먼 박사는 내 병명을 진단해내지 못했다.
I developed an online test to diagnose depression.
나는 우울증 진단을 위한 온라인 테스트를 개발했다.

---

artificial
[à:rtəfíʃəl]
혱 인공의, 인공적인
(= unnatural)

artificial light 인공 조명
an **artificial** satellite 인공위성

This street is bright at night due to artificial light.
이 거리는 인공 조명 때문에 밤에 밝다.
People often mistake an artificial satellite for a star.
사람들은 종종 인공위성을 별로 착각한다.

---

inquire
[inkwáiər]
통 문의하다; 조사하다

▶ inquiry
혱 문의; 조사

inquire about ~에 대해 문의하다
inquire into ~에 대해 조사하다

I have inquired about the computer course.
나는 그 컴퓨터 강좌에 대해 문의했다.
Police are inquiring into the cause of the incident.
경찰이 그 사건의 원인을 조사하고 있다.

---

qualification
[kwὰləfəkéiʃən]
혱 자격 요건, 자격

▶ qualify
통 자격을 주다

a **qualification** process 자격 검증 과정
an academic **qualification** 학업적 자격 요건

Alice went through the teacher qualification process.
앨리스는 교사 자격 검증 과정을 거쳤다.
The firm requires no academic qualifications to enter.
그 회사는 입사하는데 학업적 자격 요건들을 요구하지 않는다.

Unit 02 유대인의 결혼

LET'S STUDY

convert
[kánvə:rt]
동 개종하다, 전환하다
▶ conversion
명 개종, 전환

convert to Judaism 유대교로 개종하다
convert A into B A를 B로 전환하다

Jenny finally decided to convert to Judaism.
제니는 마침내 유대교로 개종하기로 결심했다.
Margaret plans to convert the hospital into a hotel.
마가렛은 그 병원을 호텔로 전환할 계획이다.

---

conservative
[kənsə́:rvətiv]
형 보수적인
 (= old-fashioned)
명 보수주의자

a **conservative** view 보수적인 견해
a **conservative** party 보수당

We have a conservative view on transsexuals.
우리는 트렌스젠더에 대해 보수적인 견해를 가지고 있다.
Karen is a supporter of the conservative party.
카렌은 보수당 지지자이다.

---

pious
[páiəs]
형 신앙심 깊은(= devout);
 실현되기 힘든
 (= unrealizable)

a **pious** woman 신앙심 깊은 여성
a **pious** hope 헛된 희망

A pious woman like Paige wouldn't do such a thing.
페이지처럼 신앙심 깊은 여성이 그런 일을 할 리 없다.
I had a pious hope that he would come back.
나는 그가 돌아오리라는 헛된 희망을 가지고 있었다.

---

violate
[váiəlèit]
동 위반하다, 침해하다
▶ violation
명 위반, 위법

violate a rule 규칙을 위반하다
violate human rights 인권을 침해하다

Anna should be punished for violating school rules.
안나는 학교 교칙을 어긴 것에 대해 벌을 받아야 한다.
Some countries still violate human rights severely.
일부 나라들은 아직도 인권을 심하게 침해한다.

---

refrain
[rifréin]
동 그만두다, 자제하다
 (= forbear)

refrain from talking 이야기 하는 것을 그만두다
refrain from violence 폭력을 자제하다

You have to refrain from talking about death.
당신은 죽음에 대해 이야기하는 것을 그만둬야 한다.
Students must refrain from violence at school.
학생들은 학교에서 폭력을 자제해야 한다.

Unit 03 캐롤의 아버지

LET'S STUDY

venture
[véntʃər]
- 통 모험하다; 투기하다
- 명 모험; 벤처사업

▶ venturous
  형 모험을 좋아하는

venture abroad 해외로 모험하다
a joint venture 합작 투자 (사업)

This is the first time that I've ever ventured abroad.
내가 해외로 모험하러 가는 것은 이번이 처음이다.
The joint venture aims to drill for natural gas.
그 합작 투자 사업은 천연가스 개발을 목표로 한다.

---

expedition
[èkspidíʃən]
- 명 탐험, 원정

an Antarctic expedition 남극 탐험
a hunting expedition 사냥 원정

Lucas is busy preparing his 7th Antarctic expedition.
루카스는 그의 7번째 남극 탐험을 준비하느라 바쁘다.
The team set off on a hunting expedition yesterday.
그 팀은 어제 사냥 원정을 떠났다.

---

hostage
[hástidʒ]
- 명 인질(= pawn)

be taken hostage 인질로 잡히다
rescue a hostage 인질을 구출하다

The sailors were taken hostage by pirates.
그 선원들은 해적들에 의해 인질로 잡혔다.
The government decided to rescue the hostages.
정부는 인질들을 구하기로 결심했다.

---

assassinate
[əsǽsənèit]
- 통 암살하다

▶ assassination
  명 암살
▶ assassin
  명 암살자

assassinate a leader 지도자를 암살하다
assassinate an opponent 대항자를 암살하다

John was accused of assassinating the former leader
존은 이전 지도자를 암살했다는 혐의로 기소되었다.
Karl hired an assassin to assassinate his opponent.
칼은 그의 대항자를 암살하기 위해 암살자를 고용했다.

---

jeopardize
[dʒépərdàiz]
- 통 위태롭게 하다
  (= endanger)

jeopardize safety 안전을 위태롭게 하다
jeopardize health 건강을 위태롭게 하다

I hope you don't do anything to jeopardize your safety.
네 안전을 위태롭게 하는 건 아무것도 하지 않기를 바란다.
Excessive dieting can jeopardize your heath.
지나친 다이어트는 네 건강을 위태롭게 할 수 있다.

Unit 04 엄마의 전화

LET'S STUDY

stir
[stəːr]

- 동 휘젓다, 섞다(= mix); 불러일으키다(= rouse)

stir a mixture 혼합물을 휘젓다
stir up 고무시키다

Stir the mixture until it is smooth and creamy.
그 혼합물이 부드럽고 크림처럼 될 때까지 휘저어라.

His passionate speech stirred up people.
그의 열정적인 연설이 사람들을 고무시켰다.

edible
[édəbl]

- 형 먹을 수 있는 (↔ inedible)
- 명 먹을 수 있는 것

an **edible** plant 식용 식물
an **edible** mushroom 식용 버섯

Margaret grows many edible plants in her backyards.
마가렛은 뒷마당에 많은 식용 식물들을 키운다.

I know where I can pick edible mushrooms.
나는 어디에서 식용 버섯을 딸 수 있는지 안다.

adept
[ədépt]

- 형 뛰어난, 숙달한 (= skillful)
- 명 숙련가, 전문가 (= expert)

adept at cooking 요리에 뛰어난
adept at driving 운전에 숙달한

Emma is a perfect housewife who is adept at cooking.
엠마는 요리에 뛰어난 완벽한 주부이다.

Even though I have a car, I'm not adept at driving yet.
나는 차가 있긴 하지만, 아직 운전을 잘 하지 못한다.

asset
[æset]

- 명 자산, 재산, 귀중한 것 (= treasure)

a valuable **asset** 소중한 자산
an economic **asset** 경제적인 자산

My intelligence is the most valuable asset to me.
내 지성이 나에게는 가장 소중한 자산이다.

Crude oil is the biggest economic asset of our country.
원유가 우리나라의 가장 큰 경제적 자산이다.

perspiration
[pə̀ːrspəréiʃən]

- 명 노력(= effort); 땀(= sweat)

fruitless **perspiration** 결실 없는 노력
excessive **perspiration** 엄청난 땀

There is no such thing as fruitless perspiration.
결실 없는 노력은 없다.

I was soaked with excessive perspiration after running.
나는 달리기 후에 엄청난 땀으로 젖었다.

Review Test

1 다음 단어의 뜻을 고르세요.

1) asset   a. 자산   b. 인질

2) violate   a. 진단하다   b. 위반하다

3) qualification   a. 자격 요건   b. 전문가

4) sterile   a. 보수적인   b. 불임의

5) venture   a. 그만두다   b. 모험하다

2 각 문장에서 밑줄 친 부분에 해당하는 뜻을 포함한 단어를 보기에서 찾아 쓰세요.

> inquire   diagnose   convert   assassinate   perspiration   expedition

1) <u>노력</u>은 배반하지 않는다는 걸 명심하렴.   (   )

2) 쟤가 유대교로 <u>개종</u>하지 않아서래.   (   )

3) 반대파들에게 <u>암살</u>당할 뻔했어.   (   )

4) 아마존 정글 <u>탐험</u>도 했어.   (   )

5) 결국에 입양기관에 <u>문의</u>했어.   (   )

Answer Key

1. (1) a. 자산   (2) b. 위반하다   (3) a. 자격 요건   (4) b. 불임의   (5) b. 모험하다
2. (1) perspiration   (2) convert   (3) assassinate   (4) expedition   (5) inquire

3 각 단어를 유의어와 연결하세요.

1) stir • • a. skillful

2) pious • • b. forbear

3) adept • • c. mix

4) refrain • • d. devout

5) jeopardize • • e. endanger

4 각 문장의 빈칸에 가장 알맞은 단어를 보기에서 찾아 쓰세요.

> hostage   edible   artificial   perspiration   diagnose   conservative

1) We have a(an) _____ view on transsexuals.

2) Margaret grows many _____ plants in her backyards.

3) Dr. Norman was not able to _____ my illness.

4) This street is bright at night due to _____ light.

5) The sailors were taken _____ by pirates.

Answer Key

1. (1) c. mix (2) d. devout (3) a. skillful (4) b. forbear (5) e. endanger
2. (1) conservative (2) edible (3) diagnose (4) artificial (5) hostage

Let's Speak

Unit 1

Carol This is the picture of the baby whom my sister and her husband adopted. Isn't he adorable?

Allie Wow, he looks so cute!

Carol You can't imagine the tough times they had to go through. A doctor diagnosed them as sterile. They were in despair when the artificial insemination didn't work out. In the end, they inquired at an adoption agency. They went through the qualification process to become parents, and then finally met this baby.

Allie It's nice to hear that they are happy now.

Unit 2

Allie What happened to her?

Monica She was about to get married to a Jew, but broke up with him.

Allie Really? Why?

Monica Because she didn't convert to Judaism

Allie He must be really conservative.

Monica I would say pious. It is somewhat violating their rules to get married to a non-Jew. I think we should refrain from talking about it.

Unit 3

Carol My father spent most of his life venturing around the world. He went on an expedition to the Amazon jungle. He fought in a war in the Middle-East, and was taken hostage. Once, he attempted to get married to an Indian princess. As a result, he came near being assassinated by the opposing party.

Allie Your father is amazing.

Carol Well, since he's jeopardizing his safety all the time, as a family, we are always worrying about him.

Unit 4

Allie Mom, I'm stirring the seasoning mixture for Kimchi.

Mom Do you even make Kimchi? Will it be edible? I'm just kidding. You've become adept at cooking. I've been worried about you since I sent you there alone. Experience is the most valuable asset in life! Please keep in mind that your perspiration will never betray you.

Day 9

현실 Reality

Preview

- commodity
- genetically
- stale
- redundant
- capacity
- acquaintance
- trespass
- property
- encounter
- afford
- apparent
- insurance
- coverage
- premium
- compensate
- indifferent
- distress
- keen
- constrain
- reverse

Unit 01 충동구매 자제

LET'S STUDY

commodity
[kəmádəti]
명 상품, 물품(= goods)

price of a **commodity** 물품 가격
production of a **commodity** 물품 생산

The price of commodities is quite high in big cities.
물품의 가격이 큰 도시에서는 꽤 비싸다.
We will boost the production of basic commodities.
우리는 기본 필수품의 생산을 활성화할 것이다.

---

genetically
[dʒənétikəli]
부 유전적으로

▶ gene
명 유전자
▶ genetic
형 유전적인

genetically modified food 유전자 변형 식품
a **genetically** modified animal 유전자 변형 동물

I don't think genetically modified food is safe.
나는 유전자 변형 식품이 안전하다고 생각하지 않는다.
Genetically modified animals may not live a long life.
유전자 변형 동물들은 아마 오래 살 수 없을 것이다.

---

stale
[steil]
형 신선하지 않은(= old); 퀴퀴한(= smelly)

stale bread 신선하지 않은 빵
stale air 퀴퀴한 공기

I would appreciate even a piece of stale bread.
신선하지 않은 빵 한 조각이라도 감사하겠다.
Remove the stale air from this room.
이 방의 퀴퀴한 공기를 제거해라.

---

redundant
[ridʌ́ndənt]
형 불필요한, 과잉의

▶ redundancy
명 과잉, 여분

a **redundant** test 불필요한 검사
a **redundant** worker 불필요한 직원

Some doctors suggest redundant tests to patients.
어떤 의사들은 환자들에게 불필요한 검사들을 제안한다.
Many firms decided to lay off redundant workers.
많은 회사들이 불필요한 직원들을 해고하기로 결정했다.

---

capacity
[kəpǽsəti]
명 용량(= volume); 능력(= ability)

a storage **capacity** 저장 용량
a human **capacity** 인간의 능력

This new USB has a high storage capacity.
이 새로운 USB는 많은 저장 용량을 가지고 있다.
Memorizing all of these is beyond human capacity.
이 모든 것들을 기억하는 것은 인간의 능력 밖이다.

Unit 02 담장 너머

LET'S STUDY

acquaintance
[əkwéintəns]

몡 아는 사람, 지인

▶ acquaint
  통 알게 하다

make acquaintance of ~와 아는 사이가 되다
renew acquaintance with ~와 친분을 되살리다

Amanda made the acquaintance of the president.
아만다는 대통령과 아는 사이가 되었다.
I'd like to renew acquaintances with my classmates.
나는 반 친구들과의 친분을 되살리고 싶다.

---

trespass
[tréspəs]

통 무단 침입하다
  (= break into)
몡 무단 침입(= intrusion)

No Trespassing 출입 금지
trespass on ~을 무단 침입하다

The garden was posted with 'No Trespassing' signs.
그 정원은 출입 금지 표지들이 붙여져 있었다.
Daniel was fined for trespassing on a military base.
대니얼은 군사기지에 무단 침입하여 벌금을 물었다.

---

property
[prɑ́pərti]

몡 소유물(= belongings),
  재산(= wealth)

private property 사유 재산
public property 공공 재산

The villa in Malibu is my private property.
말리부에 있는 휴가용 주택은 내 사유 재산이다.
Public property should be protected by everyone.
공공 재산은 모두에게 보호받아야 한다.

---

encounter
[inkáuntər]

통 우연히 만나다
  (= run into),
  맞닥뜨리다(= face)
몡 우연한 만남, 마주침

encounter a problem 문제에 맞닥뜨리다
a brief encounter 짧은 만남

I've never encountered the problem of drug addiction.
나는 약물 중독 문제에 맞닥뜨린 적이 없다.
The brief encounter with him has changed my life.
그와의 짧은 만남이 내 인생을 바꾸었다.

---

afford
[əfɔ́ːrd]

통 살 수 있다,
  지불할 수 있다

▶ affordable
  형 가격이 적당한

afford a car 차를 살 수 있다
afford the rent 임대료를 지불할 수 있다

I'll be able to afford the car next year.
나는 내년에 그 차를 살 수 있을 것이다.
Amy couldn't afford the rent on her office this month.
에이미는 이번 달에 사무실 임대료를 지불할 수 없었다.

Unit 03 추억을 잃다

LET'S STUDY

apparent
[əpǽrənt]
- 형 분명한, 명백한
  (= manifest)

an **apparent** reason 분명한 이유
an **apparent** failure 명백한 실패

Mila made a call to Leo for no apparent reason.
밀라는 분명한 이유 없이 레오에게 전화를 걸었다.
I will take full responsibility for the apparent failure.
내가 이 명백한 실패에 대한 모든 책임을 지겠다.

---

insurance
[inʃú(:)ərəns]
- 명 보험(= assurance)

travel **insurance** 여행 보험
health **insurance** 건강 보험

You need to take out travel insurance now.
당신은 지금 여행 보험에 들어야 한다.
Thanks to health insurance, I'm now under treatment.
건강 보험 덕분에 나는 지금 치료 중이다.

---

coverage
[kʌ́vəridʒ]
- 명 보상 범위; 보도

▶ cover
- 동 보상하다; 덮다

insurance **coverage** 보험 보상 범위
press **coverage** 언론 보도

My insurance coverage is smaller than yours.
내 보험의 보상 범위는 당신 것보다 적다.
The big scandal attracted wide press coverage.
그 엄청난 스캔들은 많은 언론 보도를 이끌었다.

---

premium
[prí:miəm]
- 명 보험료, 할증료
  (= payment)
- 형 최고급의
  (= superlative)

insurance **premium** 보험료
premium quality 최고급 품질

I can help reduce your insurance premium by 50%.
나는 당신의 보험료가 50%까지 줄어들도록 도울 수 있다.
The teahouse only offers premium quality tea.
이 찻집은 최고급 품질의 차만을 제공한다.

---

compensate
[kámpənsèit]
- 동 보상하다

▶ compensation
- 명 보상

compensate for ~을 보상하다
compensate a victim 희생자에게 보상하다

Money can't compensate for the loss of life.
돈이 인명 손실을 보상할 수는 없다.
No one has compensated the victims of the accident.
아무도 그 사고의 희생자들에게 보상하지 않았다.

Unit 04 소원해진 관계

LET'S STUDY

indifferent
[indífərənt]

형 무관심한(= apathetic)

indifferent to religion 종교에 무관심한
indifferent to success 성공에 무관심한

Charlotte is completely indifferent to religion.
샬롯은 종교에는 전혀 무관심하다.
I know that Leo pretends to be indifferent to success.
나는 레오가 성공에 무관심한 척한다는 걸 알고 있다.

distress
[distrés]

동 괴롭히다(= hurt)
명 괴로움(= suffering)

distress oneself by ~하면서 자신을 괴롭히다
cause distress to ~에게 괴로움을 주다

Do not distress yourself by regretting the past.
과거를 후회하면서 자신을 괴롭히지 마라.
His behavior caused much distress to other coworkers.
그의 행동은 다른 동료들에게 많은 괴로움을 주었다.

keen
[ki:n]

형 열중하는; 날카로운

▶ keenly
부 열심히; 날카롭게

be keen on studying 공부에 열중하다
be keen on discussing 논의에 열중하다

Anna is keen on studying French nowadays.
안나는 요즘 프랑스어 공부에 열중하고 있다.
The executives are still keen on discussing the subject.
경영자들은 여전히 그 주제 논의에 열중하고 있다.

constrain
[kənstréin]

동 구속하다(= bind);
강요하다(= force)

constrain a behavior 행동을 구속하다
constrain freedom 자유를 구속하다

The rules are made to constrain certain behaviors.
그 규칙들은 특정 행동들을 구속하기 위해 만들어졌다.
No one can constrain my freedom of conscience.
누구도 내 양심의 자유를 구속할 수 없다.

reverse
[rivə́:rs]

동 뒤바꾸다(= turn)
명 반대(= contrary)
형 반대의(= opposite)

reverse an idea 생각을 바꾸다
reverse an decision 결정을 번복하다

Mrs. Spenser has reversed her ideas on politics.
스펜서 부인은 정치에 대한 그녀의 생각을 바꾸었다.
Jake won't reverse his decision to get married to Mila.
제이크는 밀라와 결혼하기로 한 결정을 번복하지 않을 것이다.

Review Test

1 다음 단어의 뜻을 고르세요.

1) reverse   a. 뒤바꾸다   b. 살 수 있다

2) keen   a. 열중하는   b. 불필요한

3) trespass   a. 구속하다   b. 무단 침입하다

4) capacity   a. 용량   b. 상품

5) encounter   a. 보상하다   b. 우연히 만나다

2 각 문장에서 밑줄 친 부분에 해당하는 뜻을 포함한 단어를 보기에서 찾아 쓰세요.

> genetically   insurance   coverage   premium   acquaintance   distress

1) 여행자 <u>보험</u>은 가입했어?   (   )

2) 이건 <u>유전적으로</u> 변형된 식품이야.   (   )

3) <u>보험료</u>가 얼마 안 해서 가입은 했어.   (   )

4) 너무 스스로를 <u>괴롭히지는</u> 마.   (   )

5) 주변을 걸어다니면 귀족들과 <u>아는 사람</u>이 되려나?   (   )

Answer Key
1. (1) a. 뒤바꾸다 (2) a. 열중하는 (3) b. 무단 침입하다 (4) a. 용량 (5) b. 우연히 만나다
2. (1) insurance (2) genetically (3) premium (4) distress (5) acquaintance

3 각 단어를 유의어와 연결하세요.

1) commodity •   • a. manifest

2) stale •   • b. apathetic

3) apparent •   • c. belongings

4) property •   • d. goods

5) indifferent •   • e. old

4 각 문장의 빈칸에 가장 알맞은 단어를 보기에서 찾아 쓰세요.

> distress   constrain   redundant   coverage   compensate   afford

1) I'll be able to _____ the car next year.

2) My insurance _____ is smaller than yours.

3) The rules are made to _____ certain behaviors.

4) Some doctors suggest _____ tests to patients.

5) Money can't _____ for the loss of life.

Answer Key
1. (1) d. goods (2) e. old (3) a. manifest (4) c. belongings (5) b. apathetic
2. (1) afford (2) coverage (3) constrain (4) redundant (5) compensate

Let's Speak

Unit 1

Allie (It's a relief that the price of commodities here is not that different from that of Korea.) This is genetically modified food, and this vegetable is cheap but stale. (I overcame my temptation of impulsive buying today. I didn't buy anything redundant. Anyway, the capacity of my refrigerator is too small to put other things inside.)

Unit 2

Allie Wow! This is a really big mansion. If I walk around like in a movie, will I be an acquaintance of nobles?
Yang Only if you are born again!
Allie That's too cruel!
Yang No Trespassing. From here, this is the private property of a noble. Is there any chance we will encounter them easily?
Allie If I become super rich, could I afford this kind of mansion?

Unit 3

Monica Did you find your lost camera?
Allie Not really. It's apparent that somebody just took it.
Monica Did you get travel insurance? Check your insurance coverage.
Allie I bought it because the insurance premium was not that expensive, but money can't compensate for the lost pictures.

Unit 4

Monica I feel like Julio is acting indifferent these days.
Allie (Have you been seeing each other again?) Don't distress yourself too much. I heard that he is keen on studying to pass the CAE exam. It might be difficult for him to care about his love life at this moment.
Monica Right. At least, it's better than having him constrain me all the time. I'll try to reverse my ideas.

Day 10

위기 Crisis

Preview

- breeding
- subsist
- improper
- shabby
- transform
- withdraw
- account
- loan
- accrue
- frugal
- launch
- retail
- bulk
- margin
- tariff
- fatigue
- criminal
- assault
- retrieve
- alert

Unit 01 아이의 발언

LET'S STUDY

breeding
[bríːdiŋ]
명 가정 교육; 교배

▶ breed
동 가르치다; 번식시키다
명 품종

good **breeding** 좋은 가정 교육
selective **breeding** 선택 번식

Sam wants to marry a person of good breeding.
샘은 좋은 가정 교육을 받은 사람과 결혼하고 싶어 한다.
My dog was born through selective breeding.
내 개는 선택 번식에 의해 태어났다.

subsist
[səbsíst]
동 근근이 살아가다

▶ subsistence
명 생존

subsist on welfare 복지수당으로 연명하다
subsist on charity 자선으로 연명하다

Many elderly people in our country subsist on welfare.
우리나라의 많은 노인들이 복지수당으로 연명한다.
The beggar subsists on the charity of others.
그 거지는 다른 사람들의 자선으로 연명한다.

improper
[imprápər]
형 버릇없는; 부적절한

▶ improperly
부 버릇없이; 부적절하게

improper behavior 버릇없는 행동
improper relationship 부적절한 관계

We do not allow any improper behavior on campus.
우리는 교내에서 어떤 버릇없는 행동도 용납하지 않는다.
John had an improper relationship with his secretary.
존은 그의 비서와 부적절한 관계를 가졌다.

shabby
[ʃǽbi]
형 초라한, 허름한
(= ragged)

shabby clothes 허름한 옷
shabby apartment 허름한 아파트

A boy in shabby clothes is sleeping in the street.
허름한 옷을 입은 소년이 거리에서 자고 있다.
I don't want to show my shabby apartment to her.
나는 그녀에게 내 허름한 아파트를 보여주고 싶지 않다.

transform
[trænsfɔ́ːrm]
동 바꾸다, 변형하다

▶ transformation
명 변화, 변형

transform appearance 외모를 바꾸다
transform A into B A를 B로 바꾸다

The heavy make-up transformed my appearance.
그 두꺼운 화장이 내 외모를 바꾸었다.
Mark is going to transform his house into an atelier.
마크는 그의 집을 작업장으로 바꿀 것이다

Unit 02 마이너스 통장

LET'S STUDY

withdraw
[wiðdrɔ́ː]
⑤ 인출하다; 취소하다

▶ withdrawal
  ⑲ 인출; 취소

withdraw money 돈을 인출하다
withdraw support 지원을 취소하다

Julia is withdrawing money from an ATM.
줄리아는 현금 자동 인출기에서 돈을 인출하고 있다.
They decided to withdraw their support for the player.
그들은 그 선수에 대한 지원을 취소하기로 결정했다.

account
[əkáunt]
⑲ 계좌; 설명
⑤ 설명하다

▶ accountant
  ⑲ 회계원

a bank **account** 은행 계좌
a full **account** 전체적인 설명

Fill out the form if you want to open a bank account.
은행 계좌 개설을 원하시면 신청서를 작성해주세요.
Celine gave me a full account of the accident.
셀린이 그 사고의 전말을 내게 알려주었다.

loan
[loun]
⑲ 빚, 대출(= debt)
⑤ 빌려주다(= lend)

a personal **loan** 개인 대출
an interest-free **loan** 무이자 대출

Susan finally paid off her personal loan.
수잔은 마침내 개인 대출을 모두 갚았다.
The bank offers an interest-free loan to students.
그 은행은 학생들에게 무이자 대출을 제공한다.

accrue
[əkrúː]
⑤ 누적하다(= increase); 생기다

interest **accrues** 이자가 누적되다
a benefit **accrues** 혜택이 생기다

High interest will accrue on the loan from next month.
다음달부터 그 대출에 대해 높은 이자가 누적될 것이다.
Real benefits will accrue to the citizens.
시민들에게 진정한 혜택이 생길 것이다.

frugal
[frúːgəl]
⑱ 절약하는(= sparing); 소박한(= simple)

a **frugal** life 절약하는 생활
a **frugal** meal 소박한 식사

Thomas has lived a frugal life since graduation.
토마스는 졸업 이후부터 절약하는 생활을 해왔다.
I had a frugal meal of potato and soup for dinner.
나는 저녁으로 감자와 수프로 된 소박한 식사를 했다.

Unit 03 보따리 장사

LET'S STUDY

launch [lɔːntʃ]
- 동 시작하다(= initiate)
- 명 시작하기, 착수하기

launch a business 사업을 시작하다
launch a campaign 캠페인을 시작하다

Karen is going to launch her own business in May.
카렌은 5월에 자신의 사업을 시작할 것이다.
We launched a campaign to encourage childbirth.
우리는 출산 장려를 위한 캠페인을 시작했다.

---

retail [ríːteil]
- 명 소매
- 형 소매의
- 동 소매하다(= sell)

retail business 소매 사업
retail market 소매 시장

Mark has been in the retail business for 25 years.
마크는 소매 사업에 25년 동안 종사했다.
There is a big retail market next to the city hall.
시청 옆에 큰 소매 시장이 있다.

---

bulk [bʌlk]
- 명 대량; 대부분

▶ **bulky**
- 형 부피가 큰

a **bulk** purchase 대량 구매
a **bulk** order 대량 주문

I can offer large discounts on bulk purchases.
대량 구입시 많은 할인을 해줄 수 있다.
Asher has placed a bulk order for the new product.
애셔는 그 신제품을 대량 주문했다.

---

margin [máːrdʒin]
- 명 폭; 여백; 차익

▶ **marginal**
- 형 최소한의, 미미한

a profit **margin** 이윤 폭
a gross **margin** 총 매매 차익

Jake sold the item with a huge profit margin.
제이크는 그 물품을 엄청난 이윤을 남기고 팔았다.
Our gross margin continued to increase to 40%.
우리의 총 매매 차익은 40%까지 계속 올라갔다.

---

tariff [tǽrif]
- 명 관세(= duty); 요금(= fee)

import **tariff** 수입 관세
a **tariff** policy 관세 정책

Cherries are expensive due to high import tariffs.
체리는 높은 수입 관세 때문에 비싸다.
We will continue to maintain our own tariff policy.
우리는 우리의 관세 정책을 계속 유지할 것이다.

Unit 04 도둑이야

LET'S STUDY

fatigue
[fətíːg]
명 피로(= tiredness)

mental **fatigue** 정신적 피로
physical **fatigue** 육체적 피로

I overcame my mental fatigue through counseling.
나는 상담치료를 통해 정신적 피로를 극복했다.
It was not only physical fatigue that made me dizzy.
내게 현기증이 나게 하는 건 육체적인 피로만이 아니었다.

criminal
[krímənəl]
명 범죄자(= felon)
형 범죄의

a career **criminal** 전문 범죄자
a notorious **criminal** 악명 높은 범죄자

I think career criminals are involved in this incident.
내 생각에 이 사건에는 전문 범죄자들이 연관된 것 같다.
The notorious criminal was caught today.
그 악명 높은 범죄자가 오늘 체포되었다.

assault
[əsɔ́ːlt]
동 폭행하다(= attack)
명 폭행

sexually **assault** 성적으로 폭행하다
an **assault** charge 폭행 혐의

Someone attempted to sexually assault me last night.
누군가 어젯밤 나를 성적으로 폭행하려고 시도했다.
I'm willing to drop assault charges against you.
나는 당신에 대한 폭행 혐의를 취하할 의사가 있다.

retrieve
[ritríːv]
동 되찾다; 만회하다

▶ retrievable
형 되찾을 수 있는;
만회할 수 있는

retrieve an item 물건을 되찾다
retrieve a memory 기억을 되찾다

You can retrieve your personal items on the last day.
마지막 날에 당신은 개인 물품을 되찾을 수 있다.
Dr. Clark will help you to retrieve your memory.
클리크 박사가 당신 기억을 되찾는데 도움을 줄 것이다.

alert
[ələ́ːrt]
형 경계하는(= watchful); 민첩한
명 경계; 민첩
동 경고하다

be suddenly **alert** 갑자기 경계하다
be fully **alert** 완전히 경계하다

I became suddenly alert when I heard the noise.
그 소리를 듣고 나는 갑자기 경계하는 상태가 되었다.
I stayed fully alert throughout the night.
나는 밤새도록 완전히 경계하는 상태로 있었다.

Review Test

1 다음 단어의 뜻을 고르세요.

1) retrieve   a. 누적하다   b. 되찾다

2) tariff   a. 빚   b. 관세

3) improper   a. 버릇없는   b. 초라한

4) retail   a. 소매하다   b. 시작하다

5) frugal   a. 경계하는   b. 절약하는

2 각 문장에서 밑줄 친 부분에 해당하는 뜻을 포함한 단어를 보기에서 찾아 쓰세요.

> account   withdraw   assault   bulk   subsist   margin

1) 적은 돈으로 <u>근근이 살아가는</u> 사람이잖아?   (   )

2) 끝없이 돈을 <u>인출할</u> 수 있네.   (   )

3) <u>이윤의 폭</u>은 크겠지.   (   )

4) 따라 내리면 아가씨를 <u>폭행할</u> 수 있어요.   (   )

5) 엄마가 내 <u>계좌</u>에 몰래 입금해 주셨나?   (   )

Answer Key
1. (1) b. 되찾다 (2) b. 관세 (3) a. 버릇없는 (4) a. 소매하다 (5) b. 절약하는
2. (1) subsist (2) withdraw (3) margin (4) assault (5) account

3 각 단어를 유의어와 연결하세요.

1) fatigue • • a. ragged

2) loan • • b. watchful

3) alert • • c. debt

4) launch • • d. tiredness

5) shabby • • e. initiate

4 각 문장의 빈칸에 가장 알맞은 단어를 보기에서 찾아 쓰세요.

> transform   bulk   subsist   breeding   accrue   criminal

1) I can offer large discounts on _____ purchases.

2) Sam wants to marry a person of good _____.

3) The notorious _____ was caught today.

4) High interest will _____ on the loan from next month.

5) Mark is going to _____ his house into an atelier.

Answer Key
1. (1) d. tiredness (2) c. debt (3) b. watchful (4) e. initiate (5) a. ragged
2. (1) bulk (2) breeding (3) criminal (4) accrue (5) transform

Let's Speak

Unit 1

Girl She has not had a good breeding, has she? I feel pity for her.
Mom Sh!
Girl Why? She is a person who subsists on a small amount of money.
Allie Even though she is a little child, this topic is really improper! Did I look that shabby? I can transform my appearance if I try!

Unit 2

Allie (It's possible to withdraw money continually. Did Mom send me money secretly into my account?) What's this? I have a negative account balance. Are these all loans? What? Interest on the loan also has accrued?
Yang You should definitely lead a frugal life for several months.

Unit 3

Yang She was nagging at me again!
Allie It might be better if we launch a new business. How about retailing accessories in the street. I mean, we can make bulk purchases at a very cheap price in your country.
Yang Well, we might have a big profit margin. But we will have to pay a lot of money in import tariffs.
Allie Right, we don't even have a small amount of capital.

Unit 4

Allie (My eyelids are growing heavy with fatigue. Huh? He looks like a criminal. And that is…) My bag! Please stop the bus! Somebody took my bag.
Driver Ma'am! If you go after him, he might assault you. You'd better give up retrieving your bag.
Allie (I should have been more alert.)

Day 11

사건 Incident

Preview

- interpret
- provoke
- delinquent
- clash
- victim
- culprit
- sentence
- scrutinize
- testify
- impartial
- conceal
- cheat
- immoral
- pledge
- reliance
- divert
- flavor
- blend
- attempt
- plentiful

Unit 01 희롱당했어

LET'S STUDY

interpret
[intə́ːrprit]

동 해석하다; 이해하다

▶ interpretation
  명 해석; 이해
▶ interpreter
  명 통역사

interpret a dream 꿈을 해석하다
interpret a meaning 의미를 이해하다

Naomi was trained to interpret others' dreams.
나오미는 다른 사람의 꿈을 해석하는 훈련을 받았다.
I tried to interpret the meaning of the words she said.
나는 그녀가 한 말의 의미를 이해하기 위해 노력했다.

provoke
[prəvóuk]

동 자극하다, 불러일으키다

▶ provoking
  형 도발시키는
▶ provocation
  명 도발

provoke people 사람들을 자극하다
provoke a criticism 비판을 불러일으키다

Leo's insulting remarks provoked other people.
레오의 모욕적인 발언들이 다른 사람들을 자극했다.
Jack's reckless behavior provoked a lot of criticism.
잭의 무모한 행동은 많은 비판을 불러일으켰다.

delinquent
[dilíŋkwənt]

형 불량한; 연체의
명 비행 소년; 연체자

▶ delinquency
  명 비행, 직무태만

juvenile **delinquent** 불량 청소년
a **delinquent** loan 연체 대출금

We offer a special program for juvenile delinquents.
우리는 불량 청소년들을 위한 특별 프로그램을 제공한다.
The new policy will help people with delinquent loans.
그 새 정책은 연체된 대출금을 가진 사람들에게 도움이 될 것이다.

clash
[klæʃ]

동 충돌하다(= collide)
명 충돌, 분쟁

be involved in a **clash** 분쟁에 연루되다
avoid a **clash** 분쟁을 피하다

A number of students are involved in the clash.
많은 학생들이 그 분쟁에 연루되었다.
I changed the topic to avoid a clash with my sister.
나는 여동생과의 분쟁을 피하기 위해 화제를 바꾸었다.

victim
[víktim]

명 피해자(= sufferer)

a crime **victim** 범죄 피해자
a war **victim** 전쟁 피해자

This organization is raising funds for crime victims.
이 단체는 범죄 피해자들을 위한 기금을 모으고 있다.
Many war victims are suffering from PTSD.
많은 전쟁 피해자들이 외상 후 스트레스 장애를 앓고 있다.

Unit 02 불합리한 판결

LET'S STUDY

culprit
[kʌ́lprit]

- 명 범인(= offender);
  원인(= cause)

a real **culprit** 진범
a main **culprit** 주범

Police haven't identified the real culprit yet.
경찰은 아직 진범을 파악하지 못했다.
Ultraviolet is said to be the main culprit of skin aging.
자외선이 피부 노화의 주범이라고 한다.

sentence
[séntəns]

- 동 선고하다(= condemn)
- 명 형벌; 문장

be **sentenced** to life in prison 종신형을 선고받다
be **sentenced** to death 사형 선고를 받다

Eva was sentenced to life in prison for kidnapping.
에바는 납치 혐의로 종신형을 선고받았다.
Aaron was sentenced to death for rape and murder.
애런은 강간과 살인 혐의로 사형 선고를 받았다.

scrutinize
[skrú:tənàiz]

- 동 자세히 조사하다

▶ scrutiny
  명 정밀 조사

scrutinize detail 세부 사항을 자세히 조사하다
scrutinize applicants 지원자들을 자세히 조사하다

The detective scrutinized every detail of the incident.
그 형사는 그 사건의 모든 세부 사항을 조사했다.
I'm scrutinizing the candidates' past experiences.
나는 후보자들의 과거 경력을 자세히 조사하고 있다.

testify
[téstəfài]

- 동 증언하다, 증명하다
  (= witness)

▶ testimony
  명 증언, 증명

testify voluntarily 자발적으로 증언하다
testify anonymously 익명으로 증언하다

Many friends of the victim testified voluntarily.
피해자의 많은 친구들이 자발적으로 증언했다.
Elizabeth testified anonymously for her safety.
엘리자베스는 자신의 안전을 위해 익명으로 증언했다.

impartial
[impá:rʃəl]

- 형 공정한(= just),
  편견 없는(= unbiased)

an **impartial** judgment 공정한 판결
impartial advice 편견 없는 조언

We expect an impartial judgment on the case.
우리는 그 사건에 공정한 판결이 있기를 기대한다.
I need impartial advice on choosing a profession.
나는 직업 선택에 대한 편견 없는 조언이 필요하다.

Unit 03 충격과 분노

LET'S STUDY

conceal
[kənsíːl]
⑤ 숨기다, 감추다(= hide)

conceal the truth 진실을 숨기다
conceal a feeling 감정을 숨기다

The press is concealing the truth from the public.
언론이 대중들에게 진실을 숨기고 있다.
It's not easy to conceal my feelings in front of him.
그의 앞에서 내 감정을 숨기는 것은 쉽지 않다.

cheat
[tʃiːt]
⑤ 속이다, 사기 치다
　(= chisel)
⑲ 사기꾼(= cheater)

cheat on a person 바람을 피우다
cheat on a test 컨닝을 하다

I've never cheated on my wife until now.
나는 지금까지 아내를 두고 바람을 피운 적은 없다.
Anyone who cheats on a test will get detention.
컨닝을 하는 사람은 방과후에 남는 벌을 받을 것이다.

immoral
[imɔ́(ː)rəl]
⑲ 부도덕한, 부정한
　(= wicked)

an **immoral** person 부도덕한 사람
an **immoral** lifestyle 부도덕한 생활 방식

Do not expect me to trust an immoral person like you.
당신처럼 부도덕한 사람을 믿을 거라고 기대하지 마라.
Some celebrities lead an immoral lifestyle.
일부 연예인들은 부도덕한 생활 방식을 이어간다.

pledge
[pledʒ]
⑤ 맹세하다(= swear),
　약속하다(= promise)
⑲ 맹세

pledge commitment 헌신을 약속하다
pledge support 지원을 약속하다

We have pledged our commitment to each other.
우리는 서로에게 헌신을 맹세했다.
The mayor pledged support for small businesses.
시장은 중소기업들에게 지원을 약속했다.

reliance
[riláiəns]
⑲ 신뢰(= trust); 의지

place **reliance** on ~을 신뢰하다
reduce **reliance** on ~에 의지하는 것을 줄이다

Victoria places a great deal of reliance on her friends.
빅토리아는 친구들을 많이 신뢰한다.
We're trying to reduce our reliance on your help.
우리는 너의 도움에 의지하는 일을 줄이려고 노력 중이다.

Unit 04

위로의 스튜

LET'S STUDY

divert
[divə́ːrt]
- 동 전환하다, 방향을 바꾸다
▶ diversion
  명 전환

divert attention 주의를 전환하다
divert water 물의 방향을 바꾸다

I tried to divert his attention from the issue.
나는 그 주제로부터 그의 주의를 전환하도록 노력했다.
We will divert the water from the river into the farmland.
우리는 강에서 농지로 물길을 바꿀 것이다.

flavor
[fléivər]
- 명 맛(= savor)
- 동 맛을 더하다

a sweet flavor 달콤한 맛
a fresh flavor 신선한 맛

I'm addicted to the sweet flavor of apple pie.
나는 사과 파이의 달콤한 맛에 중독되었다.
Add some basil to give a fresh flavor to the salad.
샐러드에 신선한 맛을 더하기 위해 바질을 좀 넣어라.

blend
[blend]
- 동 섞다, 혼합하다 (= combine)
- 명 혼합물

blend ingredients 재료들을 섞다
blend colors 색깔을 섞다

Blend all the ingredients with salt in a big bowl.
큰 그릇에 모든 재료를 소금과 함께 섞어라.
Zoe created a new color by blending several colors.
조이는 여러 가지 색을 혼합하여 새로운 색깔을 만들었다.

attempt
[ətémpt]
- 명 시도(= try)
- 동 시도하다

an escape attempt 탈출 시도
an assassination attempt 암살 시도

No escape attempt was successful in this prison.
이 감옥에서는 어떤 탈출 시도도 성공한 적이 없었다.
The first lady was shot in an assassination attempt.
영부인이 암살 시도로 총에 맞았다.

plentiful
[pléntifəl]
- 형 풍부한, 가득 찬
▶ plenty
  명 풍부함
▶ plentifully
  부 풍부하게

plentiful food 풍부한 음식
plentiful water 풍부한 물

We have plentiful food to share with your family.
우리는 너의 가족과 함께 나눌 만한 풍부한 음식이 있다.
Plentiful water is necessary to grow rice well.
벼를 잘 기르기 위해서는 풍부한 물이 필수적이다.

Review Test

1 다음 단어의 뜻을 고르세요.

1) divert 　　a. 전환하다 　　b. 해석하다

2) plentiful 　　a. 부도덕한 　　b. 풍부한

3) scrutinize 　　a. 자세히 조사하다 　　b. 맹세하다

4) provoke 　　a. 자극하다 　　b. 숨기다

5) sentence 　　a. 섞다 　　b. 선고하다

2 각 문장에서 밑줄 친 부분에 해당하는 뜻을 포함한 단어를 보기에서 찾아 쓰세요.

> delinquent　flavor　reliance　impartial　interpret　cheat

1) 내가 방금 제대로 해석한 건가?　　(　　　　)

2) 얼핏 봐도 불량한 애들이잖아.　　(　　　　)

3) 공정하지 않은 재판이었지.　　(　　　　)

4) 어떤 여자랑 몰래 바람피고 있지 뭐야!　　(　　　　)

5) 육수의 맛이 특이하네.　　(　　　　)

Answer Key
1. (1) a. 전환하다 (2) b. 풍부한 (3) a. 자세히 조사하다 (4) a. 자극하다 (5) b. 선고하다
2. (1) interpret (2) delinquent (3) impartial (4) cheat (5) flavor

3 각 단어를 유의어와 연결하세요.

1) testify • • a. swear

2) pledge • • b. witness

3) blend • • c. sufferer

4) conceal • • d. combine

5) victim • • e. hide

4 각 문장의 빈칸에 가장 알맞은 단어를 보기에서 찾아 쓰세요.

> attempt reliance culprit impartial clash immoral

1) Police haven't identified the real _____ yet.

2) A number of students are involved in the _____.

3) Victoria places a great deal of _____ on her friends.

4) No escape _____ was successful in this prison.

5) Do not expect me to trust a(an) _____ person like you.

Answer Key
1. (1) b. witness (2) a. swear (3) d. combine (4) e. hide (5) c. sufferer
2. (1) culprit (2) clash (3) reliance (4) attempt (5) immoral

Let's Speak

Unit 1

Allie (Did I interpret it correctly? Let's not provoke them. Even at a glance, I can see that they are delinquent. It would have caused more trouble if I had clashed with them. I heard of a Korean victim who got hit with a hammer on the street.)

Unit 2

Carol You must have been very shocked. Actually, there was a case of a torso murder of a Korean woman. The culprit was her English husband. He was sentenced to only 5 years.

Allie What? Maybe they didn't scrutinize the case properly, right?

Carol The husband testified that the wife had been hitting him. I don t think it was an impartial judgment.

Unit 3

Monica Something kept bugging me. I felt that he was concealing something, so I followed after him. He's been cheating on me with another woman! I knew this kind of thing would happen. He is an immoral bastard as ever! He pledged that he would never do it again, but I don't care. I must have placed a great deal of reliance on him. It's definitely over!

Unit 4

Monica Who's that?

Allie Monica, I brought something that might help divert your mood.

Monica Come on in. Um, the flavor of this stock tastes somewhat different.

Allie I blended soybean paste with red wine. It took several attempts to get it right.

Monica Oh, a miso soup! I also like Japanese food.

Allie No, it's Korean soybean paste, and it has very plentiful healthy ingredients.

Day 12

여행 Travel

Preview

- □ abundant
- □ destination
- □ exceed
- □ turbulence
- □ fasten
- □ invaluable
- □ impair
- □ appreciate
- □ cripple
- □ excel
- □ preserve
- □ monitor
- □ financial
- □ exclusive
- □ prohibit
- □ accommodate
- □ vehicle
- □ livelihood
- □ submerge
- □ struggle

Unit 01 모니카의 고향

LET'S STUDY

abundant
[əbʌ́ndənt]
혱 풍부한(= ample)

abundant food 풍부한 음식
abundant water 충분한 물

I've prepared abundant food for the party tonight.
나는 오늘 밤 파티를 위해서 충분한 음식을 준비했다.
People moved to the areas with abundant water.
사람들은 풍부한 물이 있는 지역으로 이동했다.

destination
[dèstənéiʃən]
몡 목적지, 목적

▶ destine
   동 예정해 두다

final **destination** 최종 목적지
holiday **destination** 휴양지

The night coach* arrived at the final destination.
그 야간 버스는 최종 목적지에 도착했다.
The Maldives are a great holiday destination.
몰디브는 멋진 휴양지이다.

*coach (장거리용 대형) 버스

exceed
[iksíːd]
동 초과하다(= overrun),
넘어서다(= surpass)

exceed budget 예산을 초과하다
exceed expectation 예상을 넘어서다

The accommodation costs exceeded my budget.
숙박비가 내 예산을 초과했다.
The concert completely exceeded my expectation.
그 콘서트는 완전히 내 예상을 넘어섰다.

turbulence
[tə́ːrbjələns]
몡 난기류; 격변

▶ turbulent
   혱 휘몰아치는; 격변의

severe **turbulence** 심한 난기류
political **turbulence** 정치적 격변

The plane kept shaking in the severe turbulence.
비행기는 심한 난기류 속에서 계속 흔들렸다.
We need a real leader in times of political turbulence.
정치적 격변의 시기에는 진정한 지도자가 필요하다.

fasten
[fǽsən]
동 단단히 매다(= tighten)

fasten seatbelt 안전벨트를 단단히 매다
fasten button 단추를 채우다

The stewardess asked me to fasten my seatbelt.
그 스튜어디스는 내게 안전벨트 단단히 매라고 요청했다.
Patrick fastened the buttons on his white shirt.
패트릭은 흰 셔츠의 단추들을 채웠다.

Unit 02 시스티나 성당

LET'S STUDY

invaluable
[invǽljuəbl]
- 형 매우 귀중한
  (= priceless)

an **invaluable** asset 매우 귀중한 자산
an **invaluable** experience 매우 귀중한 경험

Sienna is an invaluable asset to our company.
시에나는 우리 회사의 매우 귀중한 자산이다.
A trip to Tibet was an invaluable experience.
티벳으로의 여행은 매우 귀중한 경험이었다.

impair
[impέər]
- 동 해치다, 손상시키다
  (= damage)

impair health 건강을 해치다
impair ability 능력을 손상시키다

The yellow dust can seriously impair our health.
황사는 우리 건강을 심각하게 해칠 수 있다.
This drug can impair the cognitive ability of children.
이 약은 아이들의 인지 능력을 손상시킬 수 있다.

appreciate
[əprí:ʃièit]
- 동 감상하다; 감사하다
- ▶ appreciation
  명 감상; 감사

appreciate a painting 그림을 감상하다
appreciate an effort 노력에 감사하다

I enjoy appreciating paintings during my free time.
나는 한가할 때 그림 감상을 즐긴다.
We do appreciate your efforts to promote our goods.
우리 상품의 홍보를 위한 당신의 노력에 정말 감사 드린다.

cripple
[krípl]
- 명 불구자
- 동 불구로 만들다;
  타격을 주다

an emotional **cripple** 정서적 불구자
be financially **crippled** 경제적으로 폐인이 되다

My rough upbringing made me an emotional cripple.
평탄하지 못했던 가정환경이 나를 정서적 불구자로 만들었다.
I have been financially crippled since I lost my job.
실직한 이후 나는 경제적으로 폐인이 되었다.

excel
[iksél]
- 동 뛰어나다, 탁월하다
  (= outdo)

excel at painting 그림 그리는 것에 뛰어나다
excel at everything 모든 방면에 뛰어나다

Thomas has excelled at painting since childhood.
토마스는 어릴 때부터 그림 그리는 것에 뛰어났다.
It's almost impossible to excel at everything.
모든 방면에 뛰어나는 건 거의 불가능하다.

Unit 03 관람객 주의사항

LET'S STUDY

preserve
[prizə́ːrv]
통 보존하다, 보호하다
(= conserve)

preserve culture 문화를 보존하다
preserve the environment 환경을 보호하다

People in this area have been preserving our culture.
이 지역 사람들은 우리 문화를 보존하고 있다.
I'll try my best to preserve the environment.
나는 환경을 보호하기 위해 최선을 다할 것이다.

---

monitor
[mɑ́nitər]
통 감시하다(= oversee),
관찰하다(= observe);
확인하다(= check)
명 감독자

monitor behavior 행동을 관찰하다
monitor health 건강 상태를 확인하다

The teachers always monitor students' behavior.
그 선생님들은 항상 학생들의 행동을 관찰한다.
The elderly should monitor their health regularly.
노인 분들은 정기적으로 건강 상태를 확인해야 한다.

---

financial
[finǽnʃəl]
형 재정적인

▶ finance
  명 재정
  통 자금을 관리하다

a **financial** aid 재정 지원
a **financial** plan 재정 계획

We have financial aid programs for students.
우리는 학생들을 위한 재정 지원 프로그램이 있다.
I need some expert advice to set up a financial plan.
나는 재정 계획을 세우기 위해 전문가의 조언이 필요하다.

---

exclusive
[iksklúːsiv]
형 독점적인(= sole)
명 독점기사

an **exclusive** right 독점 권리
an **exclusive** interview 독점 인터뷰

Sam acquired the exclusive right to use the resource.
샘이 그 자원을 사용할 수 있는 독점 권리를 얻었다.
An exclusive interview with the actress will be aired.
그 여배우와의 독점 인터뷰가 방송될 것이다.

---

prohibit
[prouhíbit]
통 금지하다, 막다

▶ prohibition
  명 금지

prohibit an activity 활동을 금지하다
prohibit sale 판매를 금지하다

Our firm prohibits any activities related to politics.
우리 회사는 정치와 관련된 어떤 활동도 금지한다.
The law prohibits the sale of drugs in many countries.
많은 나라에서 법은 마약 판매를 금지한다.

Unit 04 사라져가는 도시

LET'S STUDY

accommodate
[əkɑ́mədèit]
통 수용하다(= hold);
숙박시키다(= put up)

accommodate passengers 승객들을 수용하다
accommodate students 학생들을 수용하다

This tour bus can accommodate thirty passengers.
이 관광버스는 30명의 승객을 수용할 수 있다.
The institute accommodates students with disabilities.
그 기관은 장애를 가진 학생들을 수용한다.

---

vehicle
[víːikl]
명 차량, 운송 수단
(= transport)

an electric **vehicle** 전기 자동차
a military **vehicle** 군용 차량

Electric vehicles will be common in the near future.
가까운 미래에 전기 자동차는 일반화될 것이다.
A military vehicle crashed into a cargo truck.
군용 차량이 화물 트럭과 충돌했다.

---

livelihood
[láivlihùd]
명 생계, 생계 수단
(= living)

earn **livelihood** 생계를 유지하다
lose **livelihood** 생계 수단을 잃다

Greta earns her livelihood by selling antiques.
그레타는 골동품을 팔면서 생계를 유지한다.
Many people lost their livelihood because of the war.
많은 사람들이 전쟁 때문에 생계 수단을 잃었다.

---

submerge
[səbmə́ːrdʒ]
통 가라앉다(= sink)

submerge in the water 물에 가라앉다
submerge in a swamp 늪에 가라앉다

The whole village will submerge in the water.
마을 전체가 물에 가라앉을 것이다.
I saw a monkey submerged in the swamp.
나는 원숭이 한 마리가 늪에 가라앉는 걸 보았다.

---

struggle
[strʌ́gl]
통 노력하다,
투쟁하다(= strive)
명 노력, 투쟁

struggle for democracy 민주주의를 위해 투쟁하다
struggle for freedom 자유를 위해 투쟁하다

We honor those who struggled for democracy.
우리는 민주주의를 위해 투쟁했던 사람들을 존경한다.
I will keep struggling for freedom for the rest of my life.
나는 남은 생애 동안 계속 자유를 위해 투쟁할 것이다.

Review Test

1 다음 단어의 뜻을 고르세요.

1) vehicle   a. 목적지   b. 운송 수단

2) prohibit   a. 금지하다   b. 가라앉다

3) exceed   a. 초과하다   b. 해치다

4) turbulence   a. 생계   b. 난기류

5) struggle   a. 노력하다   b. 보존하다

2 각 문장에서 밑줄 친 부분에 해당하는 뜻을 포함한 단어를 보기에서 찾아 쓰세요.

> excel   accommodate   financial   cripple   fasten   appreciate

1) 일종의 정서적 불구자였다는 평도 있어.   (   )

2) 이 곤돌라는 6명까지 수용할 수 있어.   (   )

3) 안전벨트를 단단히 매 주세요.   (   )

4) 덕분에 이런 명화를 감상할 수 있게 됐지.   (   )

5) 조각뿐 아니라 그림에도 뛰어났던 천재였어.   (   )

Answer Key
1. (1) b. 운송 수단 (2) a. 금지하다 (3) a. 초과하다 (4) b. 난기류 (5) a. 노력하다
2. (1) cripple (2) accommodate (3) fasten (4) appreciate (5) excel

3 각 단어를 유의어와 연결하세요.

1) invaluable •   • a. damage

2) submerge •   • b. ample

3) abundant •   • c. conserve

4) impair •   • d. priceless

5) preserve •   • e. sink

4 각 문장의 빈칸에 가장 알맞은 단어를 보기에서 찾아 쓰세요.

> fasten exclusive monitor financial livelihood destination

1) We have _____ aid programs for students.

2) Sam acquired the _____ right to use the resource.

3) The night coach arrived at the final _____.

4) Greta earns her _____ by selling antiques.

5) The teachers always _____ students' behavior.

Answer Key
1. (1) d. priceless (2) e. sink (3) b. ample (4) a. damage (5) c. conserve
2. (1) financial (2) exclusive (3) destination (4) livelihood (5) monitor

Let's Speak

Unit 1

Monica   I'll have to apply for vacation, and go back to Italy for a while.

Allie   If you are okay, can I go with you? There are abundant cultural heritage sites in Italy. I wanted to make Italy my first destination if I ever travel to Europe. (If I stay in her house, the travel expenses won't exceed my budget limit.)

On Air   We will be passing through turbulence. Please fasten your seatbelt.

Unit 2

Allie   These are the invaluable ceiling paintings of Michelangelo.

Monica   His health was impaired due to the hard drawing work. Thanks to him, we can appreciate these amazing paintings. Some people say that he was a kind of emotional cripple. But he was a genius who excelled in drawing as well as in sculpturing.

Unit 3

Monica   Is the bed comfortable?

Allie   I had fun in the afternoon. Even though that was an old chapel, it was well preserved. By the way, why were some tourists arguing with the guards there?

Monica   I guess they took pictures inside. They might have been caught by the guards who were monitoring people. NHK provided enormous financial support for restoration of the drawings, so it has exclusive rights to take photographs there. For that reason, it is prohibited to take pictures there.

Unit 4

Monica   This gondola can accommodate up to 6 people. In the past, it was a vehicle for nobles. But now, it's a part of the livelihood of the residents here.

Allie   But I heard that Venice is submerging, right?

Monica   Yes, many experts are struggling to solve the problem.

Allie   It would be a shame if this becomes the last trip to Venice. I want to come again someday later.

Day 13

학교 School

건드리진 마.
sensitive한 애야.

Preview

- [ ] fabric
- [ ] patch
- [ ] spur
- [ ] stamina
- [ ] assist
- [ ] compatible
- [ ] widen
- [ ] infrastructure
- [ ] advance
- [ ] diminish
- [ ] sensitive
- [ ] domestic
- [ ] firsthand
- [ ] ownership
- [ ] potential
- [ ] commence
- [ ] agenda
- [ ] proponent
- [ ] ordinance
- [ ] restrict

Unit 01 다시 일상으로

LET'S STUDY

fabric
[fǽbrik]
명 천, 직물(= cloth)

cotton fabric 면직물
silk fabric 실크직물

Cotton fabric can absorb sweat well.
면직물은 땀을 잘 흡수한다.
This blouse is made of 100% silk fabric.
이 블라우스는 100% 실크직물로 만들어졌다.

patch
[pætʃ]
명 천 조각(= piece)
동 덧대다

an eye patch 안대
a nicotine patch 금연용 반창고

You need to wear the eye patch this whole week.
너는 이번 주 내내 안대를 착용할 필요가 있다.
A nicotine patch wasn't really effective for me.
금연용 반창고는 나에게는 크게 효과가 없었다.

spur
[spəːr]
동 박차를 가하다(= urge); 자극하다(= stimulate)
명 박차; 충동

spur economic growth 경제 성장에 박차를 가하다
on the spur of the moment 순간적인 충동으로

The government made plans to spur economic growth.
정부는 경제 성장에 박차를 가할 계획을 세웠다.
I bought this lipstick on the spur of the moment.
나는 순간적인 충동으로 이 립스틱을 구입했다.

stamina
[stǽmənə]
명 체력, 힘(= energy)

physical stamina 신체적인 힘
mental stamina 정신적인 힘

You need to build physical stamina first to study hard.
열심히 공부하기 위해서는 먼저 신체적인 힘을 먼저 길러야 한다.
A marathon requires a lot of mental stamina.
마라톤은 엄청난 정신적인 힘을 필요로 한다.

assist
[əsíst]
동 돕다, 거들다

▶ assistance
　명 도움
▶ assistant
　명 조수
　형 도움을 주는

assist a client 고객을 돕다
assist a patient 환자들 돌보다

We have many professionals ready to assist clients.
우리에게는 고객을 도울 준비가 된 많은 전문가들이 있다.
Mrs. Simpson has been assisting patients for 10 years.
심슨 부인은 10년 동안 환자들을 돌봐왔다.

Unit 02 대영제국

LET'S STUDY

compatible
[kəmpǽtəbl]
- 형 조화로운, 잘 맞는 (= harmonious); 호환이 되는

be **compatible** with each other 서로 잘 맞다
be **compatible** with Mac 맥과 호환이 되다

Liam and Eva are very compatible with each other.
리암과 에바는 서로 정말 잘 맞는다.
This program is not compatible with Mac.
이 프로그램은 맥과 호환이 안 된다.

widen
[wáidən]
- 동 넓히다(= broaden)

widen a road 길을 넓히다
widen knowledge 지식을 넓히다

Some locals didn't agree to **widen** the road.
일부 지역 사람들은 그 길을 넓히는 데 동의하지 않았다.
This lecture will help me widen my knowledge of law.
이 강의는 법에 대한 내 지식을 넓히는 데 도움을 줄 것이다.

infrastructure
[ínfrəstrʌ̀ktʃər]
- 명 기반 시설, 기초 (= foundation)

communication **infrastructure** 통신 기반 시설
transport **infrastructure** 교통 기반 시설

Our communication infrastructure is highly advanced.
우리의 통신 기반 시설은 매우 발달했다.
The transport infrastructure in the countryside is poor.
시골의 교통 기반 시설은 낙후되어 있다.

advance
[ədvǽns]
- 동 진보시키다, 발전시키다 (= develop)
- 명 진보, 발전

an **advanced** technology 진보된 기술
in **advance** 사전에

I have the most advanced technology in this field.
내가 이 분야에서 가장 진보된 기술을 가지고 있다.
You should make a reservation a week in advance.
너는 일주일 전에 미리 예약을 해야 한다.

diminish
[dimíniʃ]
- 동 떨어뜨리다(= belittle), 줄이다(= lesson)

diminish value 가치를 떨어뜨리다
diminish power 힘을 약화시키다

The scratch diminished the value of the pottery.
그 흠집이 도자기의 가치를 떨어뜨렸다.
The riots diminished the power of the government.
그 폭동들이 정부의 힘을 약화시켰다.

Unit 03 나를 봐 줘

LET'S STUDY

sensitive
[sénsətiv]

- 형 예민한, 민감한

▶ sensitivity
  명 예민함, 민감함

a **sensitive** nose 예민한 코
a **sensitive** issue 민감한 주제

I bought an air purifier for my sensitive nose.
나는 예민한 코를 위해서 공기청정기를 샀다.
Annual salary is a sensitive issue to bring up.
연봉은 이야기를 꺼내기에는 민감한 주제이다.

domestic
[dəméstik]

- 형 가정의(= household); 국내의(= national)
- 명 가정부

a **domestic** pet 가정용 애완동물
domestic industry 국내 산업

A tiger is too dangerous as a domestic pet.
호랑이는 가정용 애완동물로는 너무 위험하다.
Our priority is to protect domestic industries.
우리의 우선 순위는 국내 산업을 보호하는 것이다.

firsthand
[fə́ːrsthǽnd]

- 부 직접(= in person)
- 형 직접의(= direct)

firsthand experience 직접 경험
firsthand information 직접적인 정보

I have firsthand experience with terminal patients.
나는 말기 환자들을 직접 다룬 경험이 있다.
Susan has the firsthand information on the virus.
수잔이 그 바이러스에 대한 직접적인 정보를 가지고 있다.

ownership
[óunərʃip]

- 명 소유권, 소유

▶ own
  동 소유하다
▶ owner
  명 소유자

home **ownership** 주택 소유
legal **ownership** 법적인 소유권

Many people get a bank loan for home ownership.
많은 사람들이 주택 소유를 위해 은행 대출을 받는다.
Luke has the legal ownership of the land.
루크가 그 땅의 법적인 소유권을 가지고 있다.

potential
[pəténʃəl]

- 형 잠재적인, 가능한 (= possible)

a **potential** danger 잠재적인 위험
a **potential** client 잠재 고객

The report outlines the potential danger of sodium.
이 보고서는 나트륨의 잠재적인 위험을 요약하고 있다.
We can meet many potential clients in this fair.
우리는 이 박람회에서 많은 잠재 고객들을 만날 수 있다.

Unit 04 토론 주제

LET'S STUDY

commence
[kəméns]
⑧ 시작하다(= start)

commence action 행동을 시작하다
commence a party 파티를 시작하다

I will commence legal action against the company.
나는 그 회사에 대한 법적 대응을 시작할 것이다.

The organizers are about to commence the party.
주최측이 곧 파티를 시작하려고 한다.

---

agenda
[ədʒéndə]
⑨ 의제, 안건(= topic)

set an agenda 의제를 정하다
discuss an agenda 의제에 대해 논의하다

Mr. Wilson is going to set an agenda for the meeting.
윌슨 씨가 그 회의를 위한 의제를 정할 것이다.

We've been discussing the agenda for three days.
우리는 3일 동안 그 의제에 대해 논의하고 있다.

---

proponent
[prəpóunənt]
⑨ 지지자(= advocator)

an leading proponent 주도적 지지자
an early proponent 초기 지지자

Logan is a leading proponent of alternative medicine.
로건은 대체의학의 주도적 지지자이다.

Becky was an early proponent of the striking theory.
베키는 그 놀라운 이론의 초기 지지자였다.

---

ordinance
[ɔ́ːrdənəns]
⑨ 법률, 법령(= law)

approve an ordinance 법을 승인하다
enforce an ordinance 법을 시행하다

The mayor approved the ordinance against littering.
시장은 쓰레기 투기 단속법을 승인했다.

The town will enforce the new ordinance from today.
그 도시는 오늘부터 새로운 법령을 시행할 것이다.

---

restrict
[ristríkt]
⑧ 제한하다; 저해하다

▶ restriction
⑨ 제한; 억제

restrict choice 선택을 제한하다
restrict growth 성장을 저해하다

The new police restricted customers' choice of wine.
그 새로운 정책은 소비자의 와인 선택을 제한했다.

Lack of sunlight can restrict the growth of plants.
햇빛 부족은 식물의 성장을 저해할 수 있다.

Day 13 학교 School 165

Review Test

1 다음 단어의 뜻을 고르세요.

1) ownership   a. 소유권   b. 천 조각

2) potential   a. 예민한   b. 잠재적인

3) infrastructure   a. 기반 시설   b. 지지자

4) agenda   a. 법률   b. 의제

5) fabric   a. 천   b. 체력

2 각 문장에서 밑줄 친 부분에 해당하는 뜻을 포함한 단어를 보기에서 찾아 쓰세요.

firsthand   domestic   commence   compatible   assist   sensitive

1) 토론 대회는 2시부터 <u>시작이지</u>? ( )

2) 내가 뭔가 <u>도와줄까</u>? ( )

3) 나는 뱀을 <u>직접</u> 보는 건 처음이야. ( )

4) 전통과 현대가 잘 <u>조화된</u> 도시라고 생각해요. ( )

5) 요즘 <u>가정용</u> 애완동물로 인기가 많다더니! ( )

Answer Key

1. (1) a. 소유권 (2) b. 잠재적인 (3) a. 기반 시설 (4) b. 의제 (5) a. 천
2. (1) commence (2) assist (3) firsthand (4) compatible (5) domestic

3 각 단어를 유의어와 연결하세요.

1) patch • • a. possible

2) ordinance • • b. piece

3) advance • • c. law

4) proponent • • d. advocator

5) potential • • e. develop

4 각 문장의 빈칸에 가장 알맞은 단어를 보기에서 찾아 쓰세요.

> widen   spur   commence   stamina   sensitive   restrict

1) I bought an air purifier for my _____ nose.

2) You need to build physical _____ first to study hard.

3) Lack of sunlight can _____ the growth of plants.

4) The government made plans to _____ economic growth.

5) Some locals didn't agree to _____ the road.

Answer Key
1. (1) b. piece (2) c. law (3) e. develop (4) d. advocator (5) a. possible
2. (1) sensitive (2) stamina (3) restrict (4) spur (5) widen

Let's Speak

Unit 1

Allie This fabric is really pretty. Can I have some?
Monica No, I exerted myself to make it with many different patches. These are the clothes for the charitable theater group, but I'm behind schedule. I have to spur myself on to finishing it early. It'll take a lot of stamina to meet the deadline.
Allie Can I assist you in anyway?
Monica Not really. Can you just buy me a sandwich?

Unit 2

Teacher Today, let's talk about what you felt in London.
Allie I think this city is a good example that shows tradition can be compatible with modernity. Just one thing, I want the Tube to be improved a little bit. I hope it will be possible to widen the inner space and to talk on the phone in the tube by upgrading the communication infrastructure.
Teacher Are you saying that technology here is not advanced enough? You are diminishing our country!

Unit 3

Students The Spaniard brought a snake to the class!
Allie What?
Monica If you are interested, you can go.
Julio Don't touch him. He is very sensitive.
Students I heard that they are becoming popular as a domestic pet nowadays. This is the first time that I've ever seen a snake firsthand. It's an endangered species. How did you get ownership? Aren't there any potential dangers?
Julio (She is not looking at me.)

Unit 4

Allie The discussion competition commences at 2 o'clock, right? By the way, the agenda is peculiar. It is "Is it okay to open a bar until early morning?" Of course, everyone must be proponents.
Monica Until few years ago, there was an ordinance that bars should close before 11 p.m.
Allie They've restricted freedoms for such a strange thing.
Monica Many European countries are just like that.

Day 14

경제 Economy

Preview

- fare
- strike
- recession
- encroach
- riot
- subsidize
- estimate
- annual
- budget
- pension
- guarantee
- advent
- curtail
- conglomerate
- brisk
- lawsuit
- persist
- fundamental
- breakthrough
- vague

Unit 01 어수선한 사회

LET'S STUDY

fare
[fɛər]
- 명 운임(= price)
- 동 잘 하다

bus **fare** 버스 운임
rail **fare** 기차 운임

The bus fare will increase by 5% from next month.
버스 운임은 다음 달부터 5% 인상될 것이다.
Rail fares are cheaper during weekdays.
주중에는 기차 운임이 더 저렴하다.

strike
[straik]
- 명 파업(= walkout)
- 동 파업하다

go on **strike** 파업을 하다
call off **strike** 파업을 철회하다

The bus drivers will go on strike from tomorrow.
버스 운전사들은 내일부터 파업을 할 것이다.
The union called off their strike after the meeting.
노조는 그 회의 이후에 파업을 철회했다.

recession
[riséʃən]
- 명 경기 침체
  (= downturn)

global **recession** 세계적인 경기 침체
deep **recession** 심각한 경기 침체

This global recession doesn't seem to have ended yet.
세계적인 경기 침체는 아직 끝난 것 같지 않다.
The number of jobs dropped due to deep recession.
심각한 경기 침체 때문에 일자리의 수가 줄었다.

encroach
[inkróutʃ]
- 동 침범하다, 침해하다
- ▶ encroachment
  명 침범, 침해

encroach on territory 영역을 침범하다
encroach on right 권리를 침해하다

The scientist tried to encroach on the territory of God.
그 과학자는 신의 영역을 침범하려 했다.
The government is encroaching on our right to know.
정부는 우리의 알 권리를 침해하고 있다.

riot
[ráiət]
- 명 폭동; 난장판
- 동 폭동에 가담하다;
  제멋대로 행동하다
- ▶ riotous
  형 폭동을 일으키는

cause **riot** 폭동을 야기하다
run **riot** 거침없이 하다

The dictator's ruthless leadership caused a riot.
독재자의 무자비한 통치가 폭동을 야기했다.
My imagination ran riot when I saw Oliver there.
올리버를 거기에서 봤을 때 내 상상력이 거침없이 발휘됐다.

Unit 02 복지정책

LET'S STUDY

subsidize
[sʌ́bsidàiz]

⑧ 보조금을 지급하다

▶ subsidy
  ⑲ 보조금

subsidize industry 산업에 보조금을 지급하다
subsidize school 학교에 보조금을 지급하다

We have been subsidizing the game industry.
우리는 게임 산업에 보조금을 지급해 왔다.
The city stopped subsidizing private schools.
그 도시는 사설 학교에 보조금을 지급하는 것을 그만두었다.

estimate
[éstəmit]

⑧ 어림잡다(= guess);
  평가하다(= access)
⑲ 견적; 평가

estimate the number 수를 어림잡다
estimate the damage 손해를 평가하다

We are asked to estimate the number of participants.
우리는 참가자들의 수를 어림잡아 달라는 요청을 받았다.
I estimated the damage to the building at about $300.
나는 그 빌딩이 입은 손해가 3백 달러 정도라고 평가했다.

annual
[ǽnjuəl]

⑱ 매년의, 1년의(= yearly)

annual budget 연간 예산
annual ceremony 연례 행사

The annual budget for the next year will be cut in half.
내년 연간 예산은 반으로 줄어들 것이다.
Many celebrities showed up at this annual ceremony.
많은 유명 인사들이 이 연례 행사에 나타났다.

budget
[bʌ́dʒit]

⑲ 예산(= estimated expenses)
⑧ 예산을 세우다

welfare **budget** 복지 예산
education **budget** 교육 예산

The welfare budget continued to decline since then.
복지 예산은 그때 이후로 계속 줄어들었다.
The education budget needs to increase each year.
교육 예산은 매년 올라야 한다.

pension
[pénʃən]

⑲ 연금(= annuity)
⑧ 연금을 지불하다

a basic **pension** 기초 연금
a private **pension** 개인 연금

A basic pension is not enough for living expenses.
기초 연금은 생활비로 충분하지 않다.
I'll take out a private pension for my retirement.
나는 은퇴를 대비해서 개인 연금을 들 것이다.

Day 14 경제 Economy 173

LET'S STUDY

guarantee
[gǽrəntí:]

명 보증(= warrant)
동 보증하다

guarantee safety 안전을 보증하다
guarantee success 성공을 보증하다

The trained bodyguards guaranteed my safety.
그 훈련받은 경호원들이 내 안전을 보증했다.
I can guarantee the success of this restaurant.
난 이 레스토랑의 성공을 보증할 수 있다.

advent
[ǽdvent]

명 출현, 도래(= coming)

advent of the Internet 인터넷의 출현
advent of mobile phones 휴대폰의 출현

The advent of the Internet enabled us to use email.
인터넷의 출현은 우리에게 이메일 사용을 가능하게 했다.
The advent of mobile phones came as a big surprise.
휴대폰의 출현은 큰 놀라움으로 다가왔다.

curtail
[kə(:)rtéil]

동 줄이다, 삭감하다
(= reduce)

curtail spending 비용을 줄이다
curtail violence 폭력을 줄이다

Sam plans to curtail our spending on food.
샘은 우리의 식비를 줄일 계획이다.
Mr. Johns will help curtail the violence in the school.
존스 씨가 교내의 폭력을 줄이는데 도움을 줄 것이다.

conglomerate
[kənglάmərit]

명 복합기업, 대기업
(= enterprise);
복합물(= composite)
동 모여지다

a media **conglomerate** 언론 대기업
a multinational **conglomerate** 다국적 대기업

There are three media conglomerates in our country.
우리나라에는 3개의 큰 언론 대기업이 있다.
This firm is a branch of a multinational conglomerate.
이 회사는 다국적 대기업의 지사이다.

brisk
[brisk]

형 활발한, 힘찬

▶ briskly
부 활발하게, 힘차게

a **brisk** business 활발한 사업
a **brisk** walk 힘찬 걷기

Emily is doing a brisk business in cosmetic products.
에밀리는 화장품과 관련된 활발한 사업을 하고 있다.
A brisk walk is the best way to keep yourself in shape.
힘찬 걷기는 건강을 유지하는 최고의 방법이다.

Unit 04 이상과 현실

LET'S STUDY

lawsuit
[lɔ́ːsjùːt]

명 소송, 소송 사건
(= legal action)

a copyright lawsuit 저작권 소송
a defamation lawsuit 명예 훼손 소송

The singer has faced many copyright lawsuits.
그 가수는 많은 저작권 소송에 휘말렸다.
I filed a defamation lawsuit against the newspaper.
나는 그 신문사를 상대로 명예 훼손 소송을 했다.

persist
[pərsíst]

동 지속되다, 고집하다

▶ persistent
형 지속적인, 끈질긴

a situation persists 상황이 지속되다
a feeling persists 기분이 지속되다

The awkward situation persisted until she was gone.
그녀가 사라질 때까지 그 어색한 상황이 지속되었다.
The awful feeling persisted during the meeting.
그 끔찍한 기분이 회의를 하는 동안 지속되었다.

fundamental
[fʌ̀ndəméntəl]

형 근본적인(= basic);
중요한(= central)

a fundamental reason 근본적인 이유
a fundamental problem 근본적인 문제

There's a more fundamental reason for the defeat.
그 패배에는 좀 더 근본적인 이유가 있다.
The fundamental problem still remains between us.
우리 사이에는 여전히 근본적인 문제가 남아 있다.

breakthrough
[bréikθrùː]

명 돌파구, 발견
(= discovery)

a medical breakthrough 의학적 돌파구
a technological breakthrough 기술적 발견

This is a medical breakthrough against Alzheimer's.
이것은 알츠하이머 병에 대한 의학적인 돌파구이다.
I'll introduce the latest technological breakthroughs.
나는 최신의 기술적인 발견들을 소개할 것이다.

vague
[veig]

형 막연한, 모호한
(= unclear)

a vague hope 막연한 기대
a vague idea 막연한 생각

Kate had a vague hope of getting married someday.
케이트는 언젠가 결혼을 한다는 막연한 기대를 가지고 있었다.
I only have a vague idea of what kind of person he is.
나는 그가 어떤 사람인지에 대해 막연한 생각만을 가지고 있다.

Review Test

1 다음 단어의 뜻을 고르세요.

1) pension   a. 연금   b. 경기 침체

2) brisk   a. 활발한   b. 매년의

3) encroach   a. 줄이다   b. 침범하다

4) advent   a. 출현   b. 예산

5) vague   a. 근본적인   b. 막연한

2 각 문장에서 밑줄 친 부분에 해당하는 뜻을 포함한 단어를 보기에서 찾아 쓰세요.

> riot   guarantee   estimate   strike   persist   subsidize

1) 이 회사는 <u>보증</u> 기간이 길어서 마음에 들어. ( )

2) 지하철 <u>파업</u> 때문에 이게 웬 난리야! ( )

3) 언제 <u>폭동</u>이 일어나도 놀랍지 않을 정도야. ( )

4) 혼자 키울 수 있도록 정부가 <u>보조금을 지급</u>해주거든. ( )

5) 이런 나날이 언제까지 <u>지속될</u>까요? ( )

Answer Key
1. (1) a. 연금 (2) a. 활발한 (3) b. 침범하다 (4) a. 출현 (5) b. 막연한
2. (1) guarantee (2) strike (3) riot (4) subsidize (5) persist

3 각 단어를 유의어와 연결하세요.

1) recession   •   • a. reduce

2) fundamental   •   • b. basic

3) fare   •   • c. downturn

4) annual   •   • d. yearly

5) curtail   •   • e. price

4 각 문장의 빈칸에 가장 알맞은 단어를 보기에서 찾아 쓰세요.

> conglomerate   budget   riot   lawsuit   estimate   breakthrough

1) I filed a defamation _____ against the newspaper.

2) This firm is a branch of a multinational _____.

3) This is a medical _____ against Alzheimer's.

4) We are asked to _____ the number of participants.

5) The welfare _____ continued to decline since then.

Answer Key

1. (1) c. downturn (2) b. basic (3) e. price (4) d. yearly (5) a. reduce
2. (1) lawsuit (2) conglomerate (3) breakthrough (4) estimate (5) budget

Let's Speak

Unit 1

Allie — Why is the taxi fare so expensive here? What a mess! The tube strike caused this trouble.

Carol — It's because our economy is still in recession. British people are complaining about people from other countries encroaching their jobs. It won't be a surprise even if a riot arises someday.

Unit 2

Allie — There are many teenage single mothers here.

Carol — The government subsidizes them, so that they can raise children alone.

Allie — Wow! What a great welfare system!

Carol — I know it has a good cause, but it is somehow problematic because some people abuse the system. The experts estimate that the recession will be intensified. They say that the annual welfare budget keeps decreasing, and the pension system is also in an unstable state.

Unit 3

Student A — Is this a new gadget from Three Star?

Julio — Yes, I like the company because it offers a long guarantee period. Its reputation was further enhanced with the advent of smart phones.

Student A — I heard that the sales of mobile phones from other companies have been curtailed because of this product. The technology of Japanese companies is amazing.

Allie — This company is a Korean conglomerate.

Julio — Ah, I didn't know. Speaking of which, Korean vehicles are also doing brisk business.

Unit 4

Allie — Ah, Chef Jang, how are you doing nowadays?

Chef Jang — Not really good. I always finish work at dawn, and the boss is not honoring the contract at all. I even want to file a lawsuit against the boss. Until when will this situation persist? I might need another fundamental change. I came here in order to find a breakthrough in my life. But, it was a vague hope, I guess.

Day 15

전쟁 War

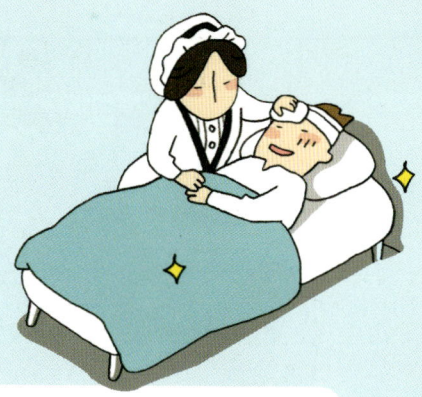

Preview

- [ ] erect
- [ ] trigger
- [ ] proclaim
- [ ] retreat
- [ ] surrender
- [ ] deadly
- [ ] casualty
- [ ] aid
- [ ] apparatus
- [ ] hygiene
- [ ] transition
- [ ] convention
- [ ] fund
- [ ] foster
- [ ] reform
- [ ] apply
- [ ] discriminate
- [ ] expense
- [ ] bankrupt
- [ ] portrait

Unit 01 크림전쟁

병원 박물관은 왜 가자고 그래?

입장료도 비싸더만

그냥 병원이 아니고 나이팅게일이 일하던 곳이거든.

나이팅게일 동상도 **erect**되어 있고.

그 간호사가 왜 그렇게 유명해?

뭐? 너 크림전쟁 몰라?

세계사 안 배웠어.

종교 문제가 전쟁을 **trigger**했어.

AUSTRIAN EMPIRE
CRIMEA
RUSSIAN EMPIRE
Black sea
OTTOMON EMPIRE

오스만투르크가 러시아에 전쟁을 **proclaim**했고 영국, 프랑스, 오스트리아가 도왔지.

유럽의 협공에 러시아는 **retreat**하다가 결국 **surrender**했어.

그게 어쨌다고…

들어봐 리슨.

LET'S STUDY

erect
[irékt]
- 동 세우다(= build)
- 형 똑바로 선(= upright)

erect a statue 동상을 세우다
erect a building 빌딩을 세우다

We will erect a statue of the mayor in the park.
우리는 공원에 시장의 동상을 세울 것이다.
Ian hired a lot of workers to erect a new building.
이안은 새로운 빌딩을 세우기 위해 많은 인력을 고용했다.

trigger
[trígər]
- 동 촉발시키다, ~하게 하다 (= spark)
- 명 계기; 방아쇠

trigger a war 전쟁을 촉발시키다
trigger a debate 토론을 하게 하다

The sudden attack from the enemy triggered a war.
적의 갑작스러운 공격이 전쟁을 촉발시켰다.
The unfair ruling triggered an intense debate.
그 불공정한 판결은 격렬한 토론을 하게 했다.

proclaim
[prouklèim]
- 동 선포하다, 선언하다 (= declare)

proclaim war 전쟁을 선포하다
proclaim independence 독립을 선언하다

The police proclaimed war against gangs.
경찰은 폭력 조직들과의 전쟁을 선포했다.
America proclaimed independence in July 4, 1776.
1776년 7월 4일, 미국이 독립을 선언했다.

retreat
[ritríːt]
- 동 후퇴하다(= pull back); 도피하다(= escape)
- 명 후퇴

retreat to ~로 후퇴하다
retreat from ~로부터 도피하다

After the battle, we had to retreat to the capital.
그 전투 이후, 우리는 수도로 후퇴해야 했다.
Alice made an imaginary friend to retreat from reality.
앨리스는 현실에서 도피하기 위해 상상의 친구를 만들었다.

surrender
[səréndər]
- 동 항복하다 (= capitulate); 포기하다(= give up)
- 명 항복

surrender a right 권리를 포기하다
surrender a weapon 무기를 버리다

Billy forced me to surrender my right to the house.
빌리는 내가 그 집의 권리를 포기하도록 강요했다.
Liam surrendered his weapon and turned himself in.
리암은 무기를 버리고 자수했다.

Unit 02 나이팅게일

LET'S STUDY

deadly
[dédli]
- 형 치명적인(= mortal)

a **deadly** disease 치명적인 질병
a **deadly** poison 치명적인 독약

The deadly disease has killed thousands of people.
그 치명적인 질병이 수천 명의 목숨을 앗아갔다.
A scorpion has a deadly poison in its tail.
전갈은 꼬리에 치명적인 독을 가지고 있다.

casualty
[kǽʒjuəlti]
- 명 사상자, 피해자
  (= underdog)

a war **casualty** 전쟁 사상자
an accident **casualty** 사고 사상자

The number of the war casualties was uncountable.
그 전쟁의 사상자 수는 셀 수 없을 정도였다.
There were 97 road accident casualties last year.
작년에 97명의 도로 사고 사상자가 있었다.

aid
[eid]
- 명 도움(= help)
- 동 돕다

provide **aid** 도움을 주다
receive **aid** 도움을 받다

Ella and Martin agreed to provide aid for the poor.
엘라와 마틴은 가난한 이들에게 도움을 주는 데 동의했다.
I don't receive aid from the government anymore.
나는 더 이상 정부의 도움을 받지 않는다.

apparatus
[æ̀pərǽtəs]
- 명 기구(= machinery)

medical **apparatus** 의료 기구
laboratory **apparatus** 실험실 기구

Our hospital has the latest medical apparatuses.
우리 병원은 최신의 의료 기구들을 보유하고 있다.
This storehouse is filled with laboratory apparatuses.
이 창고는 실험실 기구들로 가득 차 있다.

hygiene
[háidʒi(:)n]
- 명 위생, 위생 상태

▶ hygienic
  형 위생적인

good **hygiene** 청결한 위생 상태
poor **hygiene** 불결한 위생 상태

We should educate our children on good hygiene.
우리는 아이들에게 청결한 위생 상태에 대해 교육해야 한다.
Poor hygiene is the major cause of many diseases.
불결한 위생 상태가 많은 질병의 주요 원인이다.

Unit 03 의료체계의 개혁

LET'S STUDY

transition
[trænzíʃən]
명 전환, 변화
 (= changeover)

an abrupt **transition** 급격한 전환
a difficult **transition** 어려운 전환

It was an abrupt transition from despair to happiness.
그것은 절망에서 행복으로의 급격한 전환이었다.
I'm making a difficult transition to my new job.
나는 새로운 직업으로의 어려운 전환을 하고 있다.

---

convention
[kənvénʃən]
명 관습; 회의

▶ conventional
 형 관습적인, 전통적인

social **convention** 사회 관습
international **convention** 국제 회의

Each country has different social conventions.
각 나라는 다른 사회 관습을 가지고 있다.
There will be an international convention on hacking.
해킹에 대한 국제 회의가 열릴 것이다.

---

fund
[fʌnd]
명 기금, 자금(= assets)
동 자금을 대다

raise **funds** 기금을 모으다
contribute to a **fund** 기금에 기부하다

The group is raising funds for abandoned dogs.
그 단체는 유기견을 위한 기금을 모으고 있다.
I contributed to an environmental conservation fund.
나는 환경 보전 기금에 기부했다.

---

foster
[fɔ́(:)stər]
동 발전시키다
 (= cultivate);
 위탁 양육하다
형 위탁 양육하는

foster relationship 관계를 발전시키다
foster understanding 이해를 돕다

Honest conversations foster relationships with others.
솔직한 대화는 다른 이들과의 관계를 발전시킨다.
This session will foster your understanding of Islam.
이번 강좌는 이슬람교에 대한 당신의 이해를 도와줄 것이다.

---

reform
[rifɔ́ːrm]
명 개혁, 개선
 (= improvement)
동 개혁하다, 개선하다

a medical **reform** 의료 개혁
an education **reform** 교육 개혁

We need a medical reform for the good of our citizens.
우리는 시민들을 위해 의료 개혁이 필요하다.
Few teachers protested against the education reform.
아주 소수의 선생님들이 그 교육 개혁에 항의했다.

Unit 04 메리 시콜

LET'S STUDY

apply
[əplái]
⑧ 지원하다, 신청하다;
적용하다

▶ application
⑲ 지원서, 신청서; 적용

apply for a job 일자리에 지원하다
apply for citizenship 시민권을 신청하다

Many graduates applied for jobs in public firms.
많은 졸업자들이 공기업의 일자리에 지원했다.
You need to pay a fee when applying for citizenship.
너는 시민권을 신청할 때 수수료를 지불해야 한다.

---

discriminate
[diskrímənit]
⑧ 차별하다; 구별하다

▶ discrimination
⑲ 차별

discriminate against women 여성을 차별하다
discriminate against gays 게이를 차별하다

Some employees discriminate against woman.
일부 고용주들은 여성을 차별한다.
Conservative people still discriminate against gays.
보수적인 사람들은 여전히 게이를 차별한다.

---

expense
[ikspéns]
⑲ 소요 비용(= cost)

travel **expense** 여행 경비
at the **expense** of ~을 희생하여

We will pay travel expenses for the club members.
우리는 클럽 회원들을 위해 여행 경비를 지불할 것이다.
I became successful at the expense of my family.
나는 가족을 희생해서 성공하게 되었다.

---

bankrupt
[bǽŋkrʌpt]
⑲ 파산한
⑲ 파산자
⑧ 파산시키다

▶ bankruptcy
⑲ 파산

go completely **bankrupt** 완전히 파산하다
go temporarily **bankrupt** 일시적으로 파산하다

The bank went completely bankrupt this time.
그 은행은 이번에는 완전히 파산했다.
Toby went temporarily bankrupt last month.
토비는 지난 달에 일시적으로 파산했다.

---

portrait
[pɔ́ːrtrit]
⑲ 초상화(= portrayal)

a self **portrait** 자화상
a family **portrait** 가족 초상화

I want to hang a self portrait of myself on the wall.
나는 내 자화상을 벽에 걸고 싶다.
The painter specializes in drawing family portraits.
그 화가는 가족 초상화를 그리는 것을 전문으로 한다.

Day 15 전쟁 War 189

Review Test

1 다음 단어의 뜻을 고르세요.

1) casualty   a. 초상화   b. 사상자

2) retreat   a. 후퇴하다   b. 세우다

3) apply   a. 선포하다   b. 지원하다

4) fund   a. 기금   b. 도움

5) surrender   a. 발전시키다   b. 항복하다

2 각 문장에서 밑줄 친 부분에 해당하는 뜻을 포함한 단어를 보기에서 찾아 쓰세요.

> apparatus   portrait   trigger   hygiene   convention   discriminate

1) 흑인을 차별하던 시기였어.   (   )

2) 위생의 중요성을 인식한 거야.   (   )

3) 종교 문제가 전쟁을 촉발시켰어.   (   )

4) 특별한 의료 기구도 없이.   (   )

5) 그런 사회 관습을 깬 거야.   (   )

Answer Key
1. (1) b. 사상자 (2) a. 후퇴하다 (3) b. 지원하다 (4) a. 기금 (5) b. 항복하다
2. (1) discriminate (2) hygiene (3) trigger (4) apparatus (5) convention

3 각 단어를 유의어와 연결하세요.

1) foster   •   • a. cost

2) expense   •   • b. cultivate

3) proclaim   •   • c. changeover

4) aid   •   • d. help

5) transition   •   • e. declare

4 각 문장의 빈칸에 가장 알맞은 단어를 보기에서 찾아 쓰세요.

> bankrupt   portrait   erect   discriminate   reform   deadly

1) I want to hang a self _____ of myself on the wall.

2) We need a medical _____ for the good of our citizens.

3) The bank went completely _____ this time.

4) The _____ disease has killed thousands of people.

5) We will _____ a statue of the mayor in the park.

Answer Key
1. (1) b. cultivate (2) a. cost (3) e. declare (4) d. help (5) c. changeover
2. (1) portrait (2) reform (3) bankrupt (4) deadly (5) erect

Let's Speak

Unit 1

Allie Why do you bother going to the museum at the hospital?

Yang It's not just a hospital, but it is also the place where Nightingale worked. Her statue is **erected** there.

Allie Why is the nurse so famous?

Yang What? Don't you know about the Crimean War?

Allie I didn't learn world history.

Yang Religion related matters **triggered** the war. Ottoman Turks **proclaimed** war against Russia, and Britain, France, and Austria helped the country. Due to the attack from the European allied forces, the Russian army **retreated** and **surrendered** in the end.

Unit 2

Yang Cholera, the **deadly** disease, became prevalent with the start of the war. There were more **casualties** caused by cholera than by the battles. This was when Nightingale headed to the battle field to provide **aid** for soldiers. There wasn't any special medical **apparatus**, but the use of clean sheets greatly decreased the casualties. Then people realized the importance of **hygiene**.

Unit 3

Yang This led to a big **transition** of the public's views on the nurses. In those days, nurses were treated contemptuously. She broke the social **conventions**. After the war, she raised a **fund** and **fostered** medical education. Then, medical **reform** was achieved.

Allie By the way, how do you have so much knowledge about these things?

Yang I'm a medical student. I'm on a working holiday to earn my tuition fee.

Unit 4

Yang At the same time, there was Mary Seacole. She **applied** for a nursing position, but got rejected again and again because it was the time when people **discriminated** against blacks. So she went to the battle field at her own **expense**. She saved thousands of soldiers' lives, but she went **bankrupt** after the war. Now her **portrait** is displayed in the National Portrait Gallery.

Day 16

문학 · 예술 Arts

Preview

- ☐ entitle
- ☐ commit
- ☐ investigate
- ☐ evidence
- ☐ intricate
- ☐ prominent
- ☐ laboratory
- ☐ identity
- ☐ inspire
- ☐ critic
- ☐ antidote
- ☐ rational
- ☐ frustrated
- ☐ circumstance
- ☐ obstruct
- ☐ impressive
- ☐ legendary
- ☐ anonymous
- ☐ figure
- ☐ representative

Unit 01 오리엔트 특급 살인

LET'S STUDY

entitle
[intáitl]

⑧ 제목을 붙이다
  (= name);
  자격을 주다(= qualify)

a book **entitled** ~라는 제목의 책
an article **entitled** ~라는 제목의 기사

Last night, I read a book entitled *Endless Night*.
어젯밤에 나는 〈끝없는 밤〉이라는 제목의 책을 읽었다.
The magazine ran an article entitled *The Truth*.
그 잡지는 〈진실〉이라는 제목의 기사를 실었다.

commit
[kəmít]

⑧ 저지르다; 전념하다

▶ commitment
  ⑨ 의무; 헌신

commit a murder 살인을 저지르다
commit suicide 자살을 하다

A teenage boy committed a murder of his friend.
십대 소년이 그의 친구를 살인했다.
A couple committed suicide together in a hotel.
한 쌍의 남녀가 호텔에서 동반 자살했다.

investigate
[invéstəgèit]

⑧ 조사하다, 검사하다

▶ investigation
  ⑨ 조사, 검사

investigate a case 사건을 조사하다
investigate a burglary 절도 사건을 조사하다

A private detective is investigating the case.
사설 탐정이 그 사건을 조사하고 있다.
Sally went to the house to investigate the burglary.
샐리는 그 절도 사건을 조사하기 위해 그 집으로 갔다.

evidence
[évidəns]

⑨ 증거(= proof)
⑧ 증명하다(= prove)

sufficient **evidence** 충분한 증거
little **evidence** 빈약한 증거

We have sufficient evidence to send him to prison.
우리는 그를 감옥에 보낼 수 있는 충분한 증거가 있다.
There is too little evidence to support his theory.
그의 이론을 지지하기에는 증거가 너무 빈약하다.

intricate
[íntrəkit]

⑲ 복잡한

▶ intricacy
  ⑨ 복잡함

an **intricate** plot 복잡한 구성
an **intricate** pattern 복잡한 문양

This novel is an amazing thriller with an intricate plot.
이 소설은 복잡한 구성이 있는 멋진 스릴러물이다.
I loved the intricate patterns on the tablecloth.
나는 그 테이블보의 복잡한 문양들에 매료되었다.

Unit 02 외로운 괴물

LET'S STUDY

prominent
[prάmənənt]

형 유명한(= famous);
중요한(= important)

a **prominent** writer 유명한 작가
a **prominent** role 중요한 역할

The panel of judges was made up of prominent writers.
그 심사위원단은 유명한 작가들로 구성되었다.
Karen played a very prominent role in the movie.
카렌은 그 영화에서 매우 중요한 역할을 했다.

laboratory
[lǽbrətɔ̀:ri]

명 실험실(= lab)
형 실험실의

a biology **laboratory** 생물 실험실
a chemistry **laboratory** 화학 실험실

A model of a human body is in the biology laboratory.
인체 모형 하나가 생물 실험실에 있다.
I destroyed the sample in the chemistry laboratory.
나는 그 화학 실험실 안에 있는 그 샘플을 망가뜨렸다.

identity
[aidéntəti]

명 정체성; 신원

▶ identify
  동 확인하다
▶ identical
  형 동일한

lose **identity** 정체성을 잃다
hide **identity** 신분을 숨기다

James lost his identity as a Christian.
제임스는 기독교인으로서의 그의 정체성을 잃었다.
I have to hide my identity until the mission is finished.
나는 그 임무가 끝날 때까지 신분을 숨겨야 한다.

inspire
[inspáiər]

동 영감을 주다; 야기하다

▶ inspiration
  명 영감; 동기

be **inspired** by a story 이야기에서 영감을 받다
be **inspired** by a painting 그림에서 영감을 받다

This movie was inspired by a true love story.
이 영화는 실제 사랑이야기에서 영감을 받았다.
I was so inspired by the painting that I wrote a poem.
나는 그 그림에 너무 큰 영감을 받아서 시를 썼다.

critic
[krítik]

명 비평가, 비판가

▶ critical
  형 비판적인; 결정적인

a leading **critic** 주도적인 비판가
a harsh **critic** 혹평가

Alice is a leading critic of the abortion law.
앨리스는 그 낙태법의 주도적인 비판가이다.
There are many harsh critics of this new play.
이 새 연극에는 많은 혹평가들이 있다.

Day 16 문학·예술 Arts

LET'S STUDY

antidote
[ǽntidòut]
명 해독제; 치료제(= remedy)

the only antidote 유일한 해독제
a perfect antidote 완벽한 치료제

The only antidote to the poison is pine sap.
그 독의 유일한 해독제는 소나무액이다.
Kenny has developed a perfect antidote to insomnia.
케니는 불면증의 완벽한 치료제를 개발했다.

rational
[rǽʃənəl]
형 이성적인, 합리적인 (= sensible)

a rational mind 이성적인 생각
a rational choice 합리적인 선택

My rational mind is telling me that he is not the one.
내 이성적인 생각은 그가 내 운명이 아니라고 말하고 있다.
Going abroad would be a more rational choice.
해외로 가는 것이 더 합리적인 선택이 될 것이다.

frustrated
[frʌ́strèitid]
형 좌절한, 낙담한

▶ frustrate
동 좌절시키다
▶ frustration
명 좌절

be deeply frustrated 깊이 좌절하다
be clearly frustrated 명백히 낙담하다

Kate was deeply frustrated by her parent's divorce.
케이트는 부모님의 이혼에 깊이 좌절했다.
Larry was clearly frustrated by Lucy's remarks.
래리는 루시의 말에 명백히 낙담했다.

circumstance
[sə́ːrkəmstæ̀ns]
명 상황, 환경 (= context)

under the best circumstances 최고의 상황 아래서
under the worst circumstances 최악의 상황 아래서

Even under the best circumstances, some fail.
최고의 상황 아래에서도 몇몇은 실패한다.
I tried to stay hopeful under the worst circumstances.
최악의 상황 아래서도 나는 희망을 가지려고 노력했다.

obstruct
[əbstrʌ́kt]
동 방해하다, 막다

▶ obstruction
명 방해, 막음

obstruct flow 흐름을 방해하다
obstruct view 시야를 막다

The car accident obstructed the flow of traffic.
그 교통사고가 교통의 흐름을 방해했다.
The oak tree outside the window obstructs my view.
창문 밖의 떡갈나무가 내 시야를 막는다.

Unit 04 거리미술가

LET'S STUDY

impressive
[imprésiv]
형 인상적인, 놀라운

▶ impression
명 인상

an **impressive** display 인상적인 전시
an **impressive** number 놀라운 수

The impressive display attracted many visitors.
그 인상적인 전시는 많은 관객들의 관심을 끌었다.
An impressive number of birds are flying in the sky.
놀라운 수의 새들이 하늘을 날고 있다.

legendary
[lédʒəndèri]
형 전설적인, 유명한
(= renowned)

a **legendary** singer 전설적인 가수
a **legendary** actor 전설적인 배우

We invited a legendary singer as our guest.
우리는 전설적인 가수 한 분을 손님으로 초대했다.
The legendary actor passed away yesterday.
그 전설적인 배우가 어제 세상을 떠났다.

anonymous
[ənánəməs]
형 익명의

▶ anonymity
명 익명, 무명

an **anonymous** artist 익명의 예술가
an **anonymous** letter 익명의 편지

This picture was drawn by an anonymous artist.
이 그림은 익명의 예술가가 그렸다.
Someone sent an anonymous letter to the police.
누군가 경찰에게 익명의 편지를 보냈다.

figure
[fígjər]
명 인물(= person);
형상(= form)
동 판단하다

a famous **figure** 유명한 인물
a female **figure** 여자의 형상

Christina is a famous figure in the fashion world.
크리스티나는 패션계에서 유명한 인물이다.
In fairy tales, a fairy normally has a female figure.
동화 속에서 요정은 보통 여자의 형상을 하고 있다.

representative
[rèprizéntətiv]
형 대표적인
명 대표자

▶ represent
동 대표하다

a **representative** work 대표적인 작품
a **representative** example 대표적인 예

The sculpture is her most representative work.
이 조각상이 그녀의 가장 대표적인 작품이다.
Here are some representative examples of real art.
여기에 진정한 예술의 대표적인 예가 몇 가지 있다.

Review Test

1 다음 단어의 뜻을 고르세요.

1) antidote   a. 해독제   b. 비평가

2) legendary   a. 이성적인   b. 전설적인

3) obstruct   a. 조사하다   b. 방해하다

4) evidence   a. 증거   b. 인물

5) inspire   a. 제목을 붙이다   b. 영감을 주다

2 각 문장에서 밑줄 친 부분에 해당하는 뜻을 포함한 단어를 보기에서 찾아 쓰세요.

> intricate   commit   inspire   impressive   frustrated   laboratory

1) 이 그래피티 <u>인상적이다</u>.   (   )

2) 사실을 알게 된 왕은 <u>좌절했어</u>.   (   )

3) 이 게임도 엄청 <u>복잡해</u>.   (   )

4) <u>실험실</u>에서 만들어진 괴물이야.   (   )

5) 기차 안에서 누군가 살인을 <u>저질러</u>.   (   )

Answer Key

1. (1) a. 해독제 (2) b. 전설적인 (3) b. 방해하다 (4) a. 증거 (5) b. 영감을 주다
2. (1) impressive (2) frustrated (3) intricate (4) laboratory (5) commit

3 각 단어를 유의어와 연결하세요.

1) rational •   • a. name

2) prominent •   • b. context

3) figure •   • c. person

4) entitle •   • d. famous

5) circumstance •   • e. sensible

4 각 문장의 빈칸에 가장 알맞은 단어를 보기에서 찾아 쓰세요.

> investigate   laboratory   identity   representative   critic   anonymous

1) This picture was drawn by a(an) _____ artist.

2) Sally went to the house to _____ the burglary.

3) Alice is a leading _____ of the abortion law.

4) Here are some _____ examples of real art.

5) James lost his _____ as a Christian.

Answer Key

1. (1) e. sensible (2) d. famous (3) c. person (4) a. name (5) b. context
2. (1) anonymous (2) investigate (3) critic (4) representative (5) identity

Let's Speak

Unit 1

Allie   Did you guys stay up all night playing this game?
Yang   This board game is really interesting!
Allie   Oh, the game entitled Mystery Express might be named after the book, *Murder on the Orient Express*. Someone committed a murder on a train. A detective started investigating the case, but things became more complicated because of contradictory evidences.
Someone   Yeah, I think that's it! This game is also extremely intricate.

Unit 2

Allie   You've been watching the soap opera lately.
Yang   It's an SF masterpiece.
Allie   Speaking of which, there are many prominent SF stories in England. I was impressed by the story of *Frankenstein*. I especially enjoyed the part when the monster created in a laboratory became confused about his identity.
Yang   Ah, that! The story is known to be inspired by a German ghost story. The critics in those days didn't like the novel.

Unit 3

Monica   It's nonsense to see a Wagner opera without knowing the story.
Allie   Um, is the story similar to *Romeo and Juliet*?
Monica   Yes. Knight Tristan and Isolde who was supposed to be the king's bride were heading to the kingdom. But by accident, they took a love potion that doesn't have any antidote. They couldn't be rational in the face of love. The king got frustrated when he found out the truth. Under those circumstances, Tristan married another woman. Later on, the wife obstructed them from meeting again, so they ended up dying together.

Unit 4

Allie   Oh, this graffiti is impressive!
Carol   Banksy drew it. He is the legendary anonymous artist of modern times.
Allie   Ah, I guess I've heard of him.
Monica   A famous figure in the pop art field nowadays.
Carol   His representative work which brought him fame was really fresh. He put his parody work in the British Museum, but no one had noticed it for a few days. Many people say that he is a genius, but some say that he's overrated.

Day 17

역사 History

Preview

- ☐ rural
- ☐ medieval
- ☐ consider
- ☐ scenic
- ☐ stroll
- ☐ execute
- ☐ oppress
- ☐ sustain
- ☐ inauguration
- ☐ flourish
- ☐ contrary
- ☐ depose
- ☐ implore
- ☐ scheme
- ☐ successor
- ☐ union
- ☐ sovereignty
- ☐ merge
- ☐ dialect
- ☐ capture

Unit 01 리즈 캐슬

LET'S STUDY

rural
[rú(:)ərəl]
형 시골의(= provincial)

a **rural** area 시골 지역
a **rural** life 전원 생활

They promised to build more hospitals in rural areas.
그들은 시골 지역에 병원을 더 세우겠다고 약속했다.
Lucas plans to live a rural life after retirement.
루카스는 은퇴 후에 전원 생활을 할 계획이다.

---

medieval
[mì:dií:vəl]
형 중세의(= mediaeval),
중세 풍의(= gothic)

a **medieval** castle 중세의 성
medieval times 중세 시대

Julie has never visited any medieval castle.
줄리는 중세의 성을 방문해 본 적이 없다.
I'd love to time-travel back to medieval times.
나는 중세 시대로 시간 여행을 하고 싶다.

---

consider
[kənsídər]
동 간주하다(= regard);
고려하다(= think)

be **considered** to be the best 최고로 간주되다
be **considered** to be the worst 최악으로 간주되다

Amy was considered to be the best model of her time.
에이미는 당대 최고의 모델로 간주되었다.
The war is considered to be the worst in history.
그 전쟁은 역사상 최악으로 간주된다.

---

scenic
[sí:nik]
형 경치가 아름다운
(= beautiful)

a **scenic** view 아름다운 풍경
a **scenic** waterfall 경치가 아름다운 폭포

You can enjoy a scenic view of the lake from here.
너는 여기에서 아름다운 호수의 풍경을 즐길 수 있다.
There's a scenic waterfall at the end of this path.
이 길 끝에 경치가 아름다운 폭포가 있다.

---

stroll
[stroul]
동 산책하다, 거닐다
(= walk)
명 산책

stroll around 주변을 거닐다
a morning **stroll** 아침 산책

After lunch, I want to stroll around the lake.
점심식사 후에, 호수 주변을 거닐고 싶다.
Adam always takes a morning stroll with his wife.
아담은 항상 아내와 함께 아침 산책을 한다.

Unit 02 퀸 엘리자베스

LET'S STUDY

execute
[éksəkjùːt]
동 처형하다; 실행하다

▶ execution
  명 처형; 실행

be **executed** for rape 강간죄로 처형되다
be **executed** for murder 살해죄로 처형되다

Liam is going to be executed for the rape on Monday.
리암은 그 강간죄로 월요일에 처형될 것이다.
Jason was executed for the murder of a child.
제이슨은 아동 살해죄로 처형되었다.

---

oppress
[əprés]
동 억압하다, 강압하다

▶ oppression
  명 억압, 강압
▶ oppressive
  형 억압적인, 강압적인

oppress the poor 가난한 이들을 억압하다
oppress blacks 흑인들을 억압하다

A good person like her wouldn't oppress the poor.
그녀처럼 좋은 사람은 가난한 이들을 억압하지 않을 것이다.
There was a time when whites oppressed blacks.
백인들이 흑인들을 억압했던 시절이 있었다.

---

sustain
[səstéin]
동 지탱하다(= uphold);
  지속하다(= maintain)

sustain economy 경제를 지탱하다
sustain a relationship 관계를 지속하다

The entertainment business sustains our economy.
엔터테인먼트 사업이 우리 경제를 지탱한다.
I don't know how to sustain a relationship with a man.
나는 남자와의 관계를 지속시키는 법을 모른다.

---

inauguration
[inɔ̀ːɡjəréiʃən]
명 취임식, 취임

▶ inaugurate
  동 취임시키다

an **inauguration** day 취임식 날
an **inauguration** ceremony 취임식 행사

There are only three days left until inauguration day.
취임식 날까지는 단 3일이 남았다.
Many people will attend the inauguration ceremony.
많은 사람들이 취임식 행사에 참여할 것이다.

---

flourish
[fləˊːriʃ]
동 번영하다, 번창하다
  (= thrive)
명 과장된 행동

flourish during ~ 동안 번영하다
flourish under ~ 상황 아래서 번창하다

Christianity flourished during the Dark Ages.
기독교는 중세 암흑 기간 동안 번영했다.
My business flourished under government support.
내 사업은 정부의 지원 아래서 번창했다.

Unit 03 운명의 수레바퀴

LET'S STUDY

contrary
[kántreri]
- 형 정반대의(= opposite)
- 명 정반대

a **contrary** opinion 정반대의 의견
contrary evidence 반대 증거

Peter expressed a contrary opinion on the issue.
피터는 그 문제에 대해 정반대의 의견을 제시했다.
A jury found him guilty despite contrary evidence.
배심원들은 반대 증거에도 불구하고 그에게 유죄를 선고했다.

depose
[dipóuz]
- 동 폐위시키다, 물러나게 하다
- ▶ deposition
  명 파면, 면직; 증언

a **deposed** queen 폐위된 여왕
a **deposed** president 물러난 대통령

The deposed queen will return to our country.
그 폐위된 여왕은 우리나라로 다시 돌아올 것이다.
Mary is still a supporter of the deposed president.
메리는 여전히 그 물러난 대통령의 지지자이다.

implore
[implɔ́:r]
- 동 간청하다, 애원하다 (= beg)

implore God to 신에게 ~을 간청하다
implore a leader to 지도자에게 ~을 간청하다

Jane implored God to save her son's life.
제인은 신에게 아들의 목숨을 구해달라고 간청했다.
We Implored the leader to fix the problem.
우리는 지도자에게 이 문제를 해결해 달라고 간청했다.

scheme
[ski:m]
- 명 음모(= conspiracy); 계획(= plan)
- 동 음모를 꾸미다; 계획하다

a fraud **scheme** 사기 음모
a color **scheme** 색채 배합

Three criminals are involved in the fraud scheme.
세 명의 범죄자들이 그 사기 음모에 연루되었다.
The color scheme of the stained glass is amazing.
그 스테인드글라스의 색채 배합은 놀랍다.

successor
[səksésər]
- 명 후계자(= heir), 후임자(= replacement)

a chosen **successor** 선택된 후계자
a worthy **successor** 훌륭한 후임자

Edward is the chosen successor to the throne.
에드워드는 선택된 왕위 후계자이다.
Grace is a worthy successor to the prime minister.
그레이스는 수상의 훌륭한 후임자이다.

Unit 04 국기의 유래

LET'S STUDY

union
[júːnjən]
- 몡 연합(= unification); 조합(= association)

the European **Union** 유럽 연합
the labor **union** 노동조합

Holland is a member of the European Union.
네덜란드는 유럽 연합 회원국이다.

There is no labor union in our company.
우리 회사에는 노동조합이 없다.

sovereignty
[sávrinti]
- 몡 독립(= Independence); 통치권(= reign)

national **sovereignty** 나라의 주권
economic **sovereignty** 경제적 주권

It is very important to maintain national sovereignty.
나라의 주권을 유지하는 것은 매우 중요하다.

We need a plan to restore our economic sovereignty.
우리는 경제적 주권을 회복시킬 계획이 필요하다.

merge
[məːrdʒ]
- 통 합병하다, 융합하다
- ▶ merger
  - 몡 합병

merge into one 하나로 합쳐지다
merge into the background 주변과 동화되다

The dew drops on the leaf merged into one.
그 나뭇잎 위의 이슬 방울들이 하나로 합쳐졌다.

The bug was completely merged into the background.
그 벌레는 완전히 주변과 동화되었다.

dialect
[dáiəlèkt]
- 몡 사투리, 방언
- ▶ dialectal
  - 휑 사투리의, 방언의

a local **dialect** 지역 사투리
a social **dialect** 사회 방언

Betty can speak the local dialect very fluently.
베티는 그 지역 사투리를 매우 유창하게 할 수 있다.

Slang is an example of a social dialect.
속어는 사회 방언의 한 예이다.

capture
[kǽptʃər]
- 통 잡다, 포착하다 (= seize)

capture a moment 순간을 잡다
capture an image 영상을 포착하다

I want to capture this moment with you in my mind.
나는 너와 함께하는 이 순간을 마음속에 잡아두고 싶다.

I went to Africa to capture the images of wild animals.
나는 야생 동물들의 영상을 포착하기 위해 아프리카로 갔다.

Review Test

1 다음 단어의 뜻을 고르세요.

1) oppress   a. 번영하다   b. 억압하다

2) implore   a. 간주하다   b. 간청하다

3) merge   a. 합병하다   b. 잡다

4) depose   a. 폐위시키다   b. 산책하다

5) rural   a. 정반대의   b. 시골의

2 각 문장에서 밑줄 친 부분에 해당하는 뜻을 포함한 단어를 보기에서 찾아 쓰세요.

> dialect   medieval   scenic   scheme   sustain   execute

1) 자꾸만 음모에 가담해서 결국 사형당했어!   (   )

2) 강력한 삶의 의지가 그녀를 지탱했어.   (   )

3) 스코틀랜드 사투리도 영국 본토와 많이 다르던데.   (   )

4) 천일 만에 새 부인을 처형해 버린 왕이지?   (   )

5) 주변이 정말 경치가 아름다워.   (   )

Answer Key

1. (1) b. 억압하다 (2) b. 간청하다 (3) a. 합병하다 (4) a. 폐위시키다 (5) b. 시골의
2. (1) scheme (2) sustain (3) dialect (4) execute (5) scenic

3 각 단어를 유의어와 연결하세요.

1) capture •   • a. seize

2) consider •   • b. thrive

3) contrary •   • c. walk

4) flourish •   • d. regard

5) stroll •   • e. opposite

4 각 문장의 빈칸에 가장 알맞은 단어를 보기에서 찾아 쓰세요.

> successor union inauguration medieval scheme sovereignty

1) There are only three days left until _____ day.

2) There is no labor _____ in our company.

3) Julie has never visited any _____ castle.

4) It is very important to maintain national _____.

5) Edward is the chosen _____ to the throne.

Answer Key
1. (1) a. seize (2) d. regard (3) e. opposite (4) b. thrive (5) c. walk
2. (1) inauguration (2) union (3) medieval (4) sovereignty (5) successor

Let's Speak

Unit 1

Chef Jang I haven't had a proper tour because I had to work even on weekends.
Allie Is there any specific place where you want to visit?
Chef Jang There is a medieval castle located in a rural area. English people consider it the most beautiful castle in the world. People say that it's a great place to stroll around because of its scenic landscape.

Unit 2

Carol Chef Jang, we are finally here. This is the castle that Henry VIII loved the most.
Allie Ah, I saw the movie. He is the king who executed his new wife within 1000 days, right?
Carol Yes, then everyone oppressed her daughter, who was left alone. But her strong will for life sustained her. In the end, she became Elizabeth I after inauguration and made England flourish.

Unit 3

Carol The life of her rival, Mary Stuart, was the contrary. She grew up in a life filled with glories. But when she reached the highest position, she was deposed. She implored Queen Elizabeth, her life-long rival, to save her life. During that time, she kept participating in schemes and eventually got executed. But later on, her son, James I, became the successor to the throne of both England and Scotland. The wheel of fortune turns.

Unit 4

Carol The flags of the two countries were combined at that time, so it is also called the Union flag. There are many people in Scotland who claim their sovereignty.
Allie It's because they were initially different countries, and then merged together. The Scottish dialect is also quite different from British English. Chef Jang, aren't you coming?
Chef Jang I guess I have to capture this moment. This is the only dream that I've achieved since I came here.

Day 18

전통 Tradition

Preview

- ☐ costume
- ☐ lag
- ☐ improvise
- ☐ vogue
- ☐ boast
- ☐ spectator
- ☐ congestion
- ☐ diameter
- ☐ subordinate
- ☐ commemorate
- ☐ beverage
- ☐ complement
- ☐ anticipate
- ☐ permit
- ☐ feast
- ☐ vomit
- ☐ dispute
- ☐ reconcile
- ☐ curb
- ☐ astonish

Unit 01 할로윈 의상

LET'S STUDY

costume
[kάstjuːm]
- 명 의상, 복장(= attire)
- 형 의상의, 복장의
- 동 의상을 입히다

a Halloween **costume** 할로윈 의상
traditional **costume** 전통 의상

My mother made a Halloween costume for me.
어머니가 나를 위해 할로윈 의상을 만드셨다.
Jasmine is dressed in traditional costume today.
자스민은 오늘 전통 의상을 입고 있다.

lag
[læg]
- 동 뒤쳐지다, 늦어지다 (= fall behind)
- 명 지연

lag behind one's peers 동료들에게 뒤쳐지다
lag behind one's competitors 경쟁자에게 뒤쳐지다

This lesson is for students who lag behind their peers.
이 수업은 친구들에게 뒤쳐지는 학생들을 위한 것이다.
The company lags behind its competitors.
그 회사는 경쟁사들에게 뒤쳐진다.

improvise
[ímprəvàiz]
- 동 즉석에서 하다, 즉흥적으로 하다
▶ improvisation
  - 명 즉석에서 하기, 즉흥적으로 하기

improvise quickly 빠르게 즉석에서 하다
improvise freely 자유롭게 즉흥적으로 하다

There are some dishes that you can improvise quickly.
네가 즉석에서 빠르게 만들 수 있는 요리들이 있다.
When drawing a picture, a painter improvises freely.
그림을 그릴 때, 화가는 즉흥적으로 자유롭게 한다.

vogue
[voug]
- 명 유행(= trend)

the current **vogue** 현재 유행
a brief **vogue** 짧은 인기

This hair style is in the current vogue among women.
이 헤어스타일이 여자들 사이에서 현재 유행하는 것이다.
The guitarist enjoyed a brief vogue in the past.
그 기타리스트는 과거에 짧은 인기를 누렸다.

boast
[boust]
- 동 자랑하다, 뽐내다 (= brag)
- 명 자랑

boast about wealth 재산을 자랑하다
boast about a girlfriend 여자친구를 자랑하다

Mary has never boasted about her wealth.
메리는 자신의 재산을 자랑한 적이 없다.
Sam wants to boast about his beautiful girlfriend.
샘은 그의 아름다운 여자친구를 자랑하고 싶어한다.

Unit 02 가이 포크스 데이

LET'S STUDY

spectator
[spékteitər]
- 몡 구경꾼, 관중
  (= onlooker)

a **spectator** sport 관람 스포츠
a **spectator** attendance 관람객 수

There are various kinds of spectator sports.
관람 스포츠에는 여러 종류가 있다.
We expect a large spectator attendance at the game.
우리는 그 경기에 많은 수의 관람객을 기대하고 있다.

congestion
[kəndʒéstʃən]
- 몡 혼잡, 밀집
  (= overcrowding)

traffic **congestion** 교통 체증
nasal **congestion** 코막힘

I was late for the meeting due to traffic congestion.
나는 교통 체증 때문에 그 회의에 늦었다.
I suffer from nasal congestion in spring time.
나는 봄철에는 코막힘으로 고생한다.

diameter
[daiǽmitər]
- 몡 지름

diameter of a planet 행성의 지름
diameter of a circle 원의 지름

We will compare the diameters of different planets.
우리는 다른 행성들 간의 지름을 비교할 것이다.
The diameter of this circle is about ten centimeters.
이 원의 지름은 10센티미터 정도이다.

subordinate
[səbɔ́ːrdənit]
- 몡 부하(= inferior)
- 형 수하의, 아래의
- 동 경시하다

a male **subordinate** 남자 부하
a female **subordinate** 여자 부하

Some female executives prefer male subordinates.
어떤 여성 간부들은 남자 부하를 선호한다.
Mr. Jackson doesn't have any female subordinates.
잭슨 씨는 여자 부하가 하나도 없다.

commemorate
[kəmémərèit]
- 동 기념하다

▶ commemoration
  몡 기념, 기념식

commemorate anniversary 기념일을 기념하다
commemorate death 죽음을 기념하다

We always commemorate our wedding anniversary.
우리는 항상 결혼기념일을 기념한다.
It was built to commemorate the death of a poet.
이것은 한 시인의 죽음을 기념하기 위해 지어졌다.

Unit 03 크리스마스 손님

LET'S STUDY

beverage
[bévəridʒ]
명 음료(= drink)

alcoholic **beverage** 알코올성 음료
caffeinated **beverage** 카페인 함유 음료

I don't have a license to sell alcoholic beverages.
나는 알코올성 음료를 팔 수 있는 자격증이 없다.
Michelle can't drink any caffeinated beverages.
미셸은 카페인 함유 음료를 먹을 수 없다.

complement
[kάmpləmənt]
동 보완하다, 더 좋게 만들다
명 보완물

▶ complementary
형 보완적인, 상호 보완적인

complement each other 서로를 보완하다
an excellent **complement** 훌륭한 보완물

The two singers complement each other perfectly.
그 두 가수는 서로를 완벽하게 보완한다.
Green tea is an excellent complement to sushi.
녹차는 스시의 훌륭하게 보완해준다.

anticipate
[æntísəpèit]
동 기대하다; 예상하다

▶ anticipation
명 기대; 예상

anticipate the day 그날을 기대하다
anticipate a problem 문제를 예상하다

I'm already anticipating the day I meet my son.
나는 벌써 내 아들을 만날 날을 기대하고 있다.
The experts anticipated the problems of the new fuel.
전문가들은 그 새로운 연료의 문제에 대해 예상했다.

permit
[pə́ːrmit]
동 허락하다(= allow)
명 허가, 허가증

permit smoking 흡연을 허가하다
a work **permit** 취업 허가증

My company permits smoking only in smoking areas.
우리 회사는 흡연 구역에서의 흡연만을 허락한다.
You have to get a work permit sooner or later.
너는 조만간 취업 허가증을 따야만 한다.

feast
[fiːst]
명 만찬, 연회(= banquet)
동 실컷 먹다; 잔치를 하다

a thanksgiving **feast** 추수감사절 성찬
a wedding **feast** 결혼 피로연

Our family prepared the thanksgiving feast altogether.
우리 가족은 추수감사절 성찬을 다 같이 준비했다.
As many as 400 people came to the wedding feast.
400명이나 되는 사람들이 그 결혼 피로연에 왔다.

Unit 04

새해 키스는 누구와

LET'S STUDY

vomit
[vámit]
- 동 토하다(= throw up)
- 명 토함

vomit blood 피를 토하다
vomit food 음식을 토하다

Karl started to vomit blood after eating the cake.
칼은 그 케이크를 먹은 후 피를 토하기 시작했다.
I vomited all the food in the toilet.
나는 화장실에서 모든 음식을 토했다.

dispute
[dispjúːt]
- 명 논쟁, 분쟁(= quarrel)
- 동 논쟁하다

a **dispute** over money 돈에 관한 분쟁
a **dispute** over territory 영토에 관한 분쟁

Lily and Eric resolved their dispute over money.
릴리와 에릭은 돈에 관한 그들의 분쟁을 해결했다.
There are still disputes over territory between nations.
여전히 국가들 간에는 영토에 관한 분쟁들이 있다.

reconcile
[rékənsàil]
- 동 화해시키다; 조정하다
- ▶ reconciliation
  - 명 화해; 조정

reconcile people 사람들을 화해시키다
reconcile a difference 차이점을 조정하다

A competent attorney can reconcile people well.
뛰어난 변호사는 사람들을 잘 화해시킨다.
The two parties must reconcile their differences.
그 두 정당은 그들의 차이점을 조정해야 한다.

curb
[kəːrb]
- 동 억제하다, 제한하다 (= control)

curb anger 화를 억제하다
curb growth 성장을 제한하다

I always try to curb my anger in front of others.
나는 다른 사람들 앞에서는 항상 화를 억제하려고 노력한다.
We have to curb the growth of gambling business.
우리는 도박 사업의 성장을 억제해야 한다.

astonish
[əstániʃ]
- 동 놀라게 하다
- ▶ astonishment
  - 명 놀람

astonish a friend 친구를 놀라게 하다
astonish a visitor 방문객을 놀라게 하다

Isaac's sudden death astonished all of his friends.
아이작의 갑작스러운 죽음은 그의 모든 친구들을 놀라게 했다.
The stuffed animals on the wall may astonish visitors.
벽에 있는 그 박제된 동물들이 방문객들을 놀라게 할 수 있다.

Review Test

1 다음 단어의 뜻을 고르세요.

1) subordinate   a. 부하   b. 음료

2) curb   a. 억제하다   b. 허락하다

3) lag   a. 토하다   b. 뒤쳐지다

4) astonish   a. 놀라게 하다   b. 보완하다

5) boast   a. 기념하다   b. 자랑하다

2 각 문장에서 밑줄 친 부분에 해당하는 뜻을 포함한 단어를 보기에서 찾아 쓰세요.

> reconcile   anticipate   diameter   vogue   spectator   feast

1) 칠면조를 정말 <u>기대</u>해왔는데!   (   )

2) <u>지름</u>이 120미터가 넘지.   (   )

3) 누가 좀 <u>화해시켜</u> 봐!   (   )

4) 요즘 <u>유행</u>하는 스타일로 만들어야겠다.   (   )

5) 이 <u>만찬</u>을 앞에 두고 참아야 해?   (   )

Answer Key
1. (1) a. 부하 (2) a. 억제하다 (3) b. 뒤쳐지다 (4) a. 놀라게 하다 (5) b. 자랑하다
2. (1) anticipate (2) diameter (3) reconcile (4) vogue (5) feast

3 각 단어를 유의어와 연결하세요.

1) dispute •   • a. overcrowding

2) costume •   • b. quarrel

3) congestion •   • c. drink

4) permit •   • d. attire

5) beverage •   • e. allow

4 각 문장의 빈칸에 가장 알맞은 단어를 보기에서 찾아 쓰세요.

> vomit   complement   reconcile   spectator   commemorate   improvise

1) The two singers _____ each other perfectly.

2) There are some dishes that you can _____ quickly.

3) There are various kinds of _____ sports.

4) Karl started to _____ blood after eating the cake.

5) We always _____ our wedding anniversary.

Answer Key
1. (1) b. quarrel (2) d. attire (3) a. overcrowding (4) e. allow (5) c. drink
2. (1) complement (2) improvise (3) spectator (4) vomit (5) commemorate

Let's Speak

Unit 1

Monica Is this your Halloween costume?
Allie What's wrong with it?
Monica I can't see anything sexy in the costume. It's just a maid costume for historical dramas. How did you get such a costume that lags behind the times so much? I guess I'll have to improvise and change it to something in vogue these days.
Monica What do you think? I'm so talented.
Allie Thanks a lot. (When I see her boasting about herself, it reminds me of someone.)

Unit 2

Allie There are so many spectators.
Carol There will be terrible congestion on the way back home. Let's go there. You can have the greatest view when you are facing the London Eye. The diameter of London Eye is more than 120 meters. Guy Fawkes tried to blow up the parliament building under James I. But one of his subordinates blew the whistle on him, so the scheme failed. People started this event to commemorate that day.

Unit 3

Yang Thank you for inviting us.
Julio By the way, who are you?
Allie You told me to bring one more guest.
Julio I've prepared Christmas turkey. This beverage will complement the turkey well.
Allie Wow! I've been really anticipating a turkey.
Julio Wait! According to our Spanish tradition, you are not permitted to eat it until midnight.
Allie Do I have to endure in front of this feast?

Unit 4

Monica Who said you can come to my New Year's party? I want to vomit when I see your face.
People Monica and Julio are having a dispute. Can someone help them reconcile?
Allie How long have they been fighting? I guess they might burst with the rage they have been curbing.
Someone Let's not care about them. Oh! The New Year countdown starts now. They've really astonished us.
Allie What's that?

Day 19

교육 Education

Preview

- fluent
- interfere
- trial
- attorney
- coherent
- institute
- amenity
- discipline
- dismiss
- assess
- outstanding
- admission
- subsequent
- register
- scholarship
- extension
- submit
- authorize
- requirement
- accordingly

Unit 01 드라마는 자막 없이

LET'S STUDY

fluent
[flú(:)ənt]

형 유창한, 능숙한

▶ fluency
  명 유창함, 달변

be fluent in a language 언어에 유창하다
a fluent liar 능숙한 거짓말쟁이

The secretary is very fluent in several languages.
그 비서는 여러 나라의 언어에 매우 유창하다.
Fluent liars can even control their facial expressions.
능숙한 거짓말쟁이들은 얼굴 표정까지 조절할 수 있다.

interfere
[ìntərfíər]

동 방해하다; 간섭하다

▶ interference
  명 방해; 간섭

interfere with ~을 방해하다
interfere in ~에 간섭하다

Overeating at night can interfere with sleeping.
밤에 과식하는 것은 수면을 방해할 수 있다.
You have no right to interfere in my personal life.
당신은 내 개인적인 삶에 간섭할 권리가 없다.

trial
[tráiəl]

명 재판, 공판(= hearing)
형 재판의, 공판의

await trial 재판을 기다리다
go on trial 재판을 받다

The terrorists are awaiting trial in prison.
그 테러리스트들은 감옥에서 재판을 기다리고 있다.
Mark went on trial for the murder of his colleague.
마크는 동료 살해 혐의로 재판을 받았다.

attorney
[ətə́:rni]

명 변호사(= lawyer)

an divorce attorney 이혼 전문 변호사
an defense attorney 피고측 변호사

I suggest that you consult with a divorce attorney.
당신이 이혼 전문 변호사와 상담해 보는 것을 제안한다.
The defense attorney has a very good reputation.
피고측 변호인은 아주 좋은 평판을 가지고 있다.

coherent
[kouhí(:)ərənt]

형 조리 있는, 일관적인

▶ cohere
  동 조리가 있다, 일관적이다

a coherent explanation 조리 있는 설명
a coherent policy 일관적인 정책

You need to deliver a more coherent explanation.
너는 좀 더 조리 있는 설명을 해야 한다.
We need a coherent policy on education
우리는 교육에 대해 일관적인 정책이 필요하다.

Unit 02 스파르타 학원

LET'S STUDY

institute
[ínstitjùːt]

- 명 학원(= academy), 기관
- 동 도입하다

a language **institute** 어학원
a research **institute** 연구소

I'm teaching Chinese in a private language institute.
나는 사설 어학원에서 중국어를 가르치고 있다.
Dr. Porter is the head of the medical research institute.
포터 박사는 그 의학 연구소의 소장이다.

amenity
[əménəti]

- 명 pl. 편의 시설 (= convenience)

lack **amenities** 편의 시설이 부족하다
improve **amenities** 편의 시설을 개선하다

The hotels in this city lack even basic amenities.
이 도시의 호텔들은 기본적인 편의 시설마저 부족하다.
The resort has improved its amenities for guests.
그 리조트는 투숙객들을 위해 편의 시설을 개선했다.

discipline
[dísəplin]

- 명 규율(= rule); 훈련(= training)
- 동 징계하다

strict **discipline** 엄격한 규율
mental **discipline** 정신 훈련

Strict discipline is needed to control problem children.
문제아들을 통제하기 위해 엄격한 규율이 필요하다.
Fencing is known to be good for mental discipline.
펜싱은 정신 훈련에 좋다고 알려져 있다.

dismiss
[dismís]

- 동 퇴학시키다(= expel), 해고하다(= fire)

be **dismissed** from school 학교에서 퇴학당하다
be **dismissed** from work 직장에서 해고당하다

Kevin was dismissed from school yesterday.
케빈은 어제 학교에서 퇴학당했다.
A lot of workers have been dismissed from work.
많은 직장인들이 직장에서 해고당했다.

assess
[əsés]

- 동 평가하다

▶ assessment
  명 평가

assess achievement 성취도를 평가하다
assess potential 잠재력을 평가하다

The test is designed to assess academic achievement.
그 시험은 학업 성취도를 평가하도록 만들어진 것이다.
I'm assessing the potential of the new market.
나는 새로운 시장의 잠재력을 평가하고 있다.

Day 19 교육 Education 233

Unit 03 학비를 모아요

LET'S STUDY

outstanding
[àutstǽndiŋ]

형 뛰어난, 우수한
(= superb)

an **outstanding** performance 뛰어난 공연
an **outstanding** student 우수한 학생

Everyone applauded the outstanding performance.
모두가 그 뛰어난 공연에 박수갈채를 보냈다.
Jenny was an outstanding student at middle school.
제니는 중학교에서 우수한 학생이었다.

admission
[ədmíʃən]

명 입장(= entrance);
입장료

free **admission** 무료 입장
general **admission** 일반석 입장료

The participants will receive free admission to the zoo.
참가자들은 동물원에 무료 입장을 하게 된다.
The general admission for this musical is $20.
이 뮤지컬의 일반석 입장료는 20달러이다.

subsequent
[sʌ́bsəkwənt]

형 다음의, 그 후의(= next)

a **subsequent** semester 다음 학기
subsequent research 후속 연구

I plan to take the subsequent semester off.
나는 다음 학기에 휴학을 할 계획이다.
The subsequent research supported his original claim.
후속 연구가 그의 원래 주장을 뒷받침했다.

register
[rédʒistər]

동 등록하다, 등기하다
명 등록부, 등기부

▶ registration
명 등록

register for a course 수업에 등록하다
register for an event 행사에 등록하다

Jim registered for an eight-week course of psychology.
짐은 8주간의 심리학 수업에 등록했다.
Today is the last day that I can register for the event.
오늘이 내가 그 행사에 등록할 수 있는 마지막 날이다.

scholarship
[skálərʃip]

명 장학금; 학식

a **scholarship** fund 장학 기금
a **scholarship** recipient 장학금 수여자

We raised a scholarship fund for poor students.
우리는 가난한 학생들을 위한 장학 기금을 모았다.
All the scholarship recipients must attend this meeting.
모든 장학금 수여자들은 이 회의에 참석해야 한다.

Unit 04 비자 연장

LET'S STUDY

extension
[iksténʃən]
⑲ 연장; 확대

▶ extensive
⑱ 폭넓은

a visa **extension** 비자 연장
life **extension** 생명 연장

Lily is going to apply for a visa extension tomorrow.
릴리는 내일 비자 연장 신청을 할 계획이다.
I'm very interested in life extension technology.
나는 생명 연장 기술에 매우 관심이 있다.

submit
[səbmít]
⑧ 제출하다; 순종하다

▶ submission
⑲ 제출; 순종

submit a document 서류를 제출하다
submit a letter 편지를 보내다

You have to submit the document by August, 14.
너는 그 서류를 8월 14일까지 제출해야 한다.
Here is the address where you can submit the letter.
이것이 네가 편지를 보낼 수 있는 주소이다.

authorize
[ɔ́:θəràiz]
⑧ 허가하다, 인정하다

▶ authorization
⑲ 허가, 공인
▶ authority
⑲ 권위

an **authorized** school 허가받은 학교
authorized personnel 허가받은 직원

Jane has the list of authorized schools in this area.
제인은 이 지역에 있는 허가받은 학교들의 목록을 가지고 있다.
Only authorized personnel are allowed to enter.
허가받은 직원들만이 입장할 수 있다.

requirement
[rikwáiərmənt]
⑲ 필요물, 필요조건
(= prerequisite)

a daily **requirement** 하루 필요량
a minimum **requirement** 최소 필요조건

This drink contains the daily requirement of calcium.
이 음료수는 칼슘의 하루 필요량을 포함하고 있다.
I didn't meet the minimum age requirement for drinking.
나는 음주에 필요한 최소 나이 조건에 맞지 않았다.

accordingly
[əkɔ́:rdiŋli]
㉾ 그에 맞춰, 그에 따라
(= suitably)

respond **accordingly** 그에 맞춰 답하다
behave **accordingly** 그에 따라 행동하다

Whenever I pray to God, he responds accordingly.
내가 기도할 때마다, 신은 그에 맞춰 답을 주신다.
If there are rules in the school, behave accordingly.
그 학교에 규칙이 있다면, 그에 따라 행동해라.

Review Test

1 다음 단어의 뜻을 고르세요.

1) admission   a. 재판   b. 입장

2) authorize   a. 허가하다   b. 제출하다

3) institute   a. 학원   b. 변호사

4) dismiss   a. 평가하다   b. 퇴학시키다

5) coherent   a. 조리 있는   b. 다음의

2 각 문장에서 밑줄 친 부분에 해당하는 뜻을 포함한 단어를 보기에서 찾아 쓰세요.

> fluent   interfere   extension   trial   scholarship   discipline

1) 장학금도 받을 수 있겠지!   (   )

2) 네 영어가 많이 유창해졌구나.   (   )

3) 비자 연장 신청 기간이 이틀 남았어.   (   )

4) 자막은 듣기를 방해할까 봐서 빼고 봤어.   (   )

5) 내가 있던 곳은 규율이 아주 엄격했어.   (   )

Answer Key
1. (1) b. 입장 (2) a. 허가하다 (3) a. 학원 (4) b. 퇴학시키다 (5) a. 조리 있는
2. (1) scholarship (2) fluent (3) extension (4) interfere (5) discipline

3 각 단어를 유의어와 연결하세요.

1) attorney •   • a. next

2) outstanding •   • b. superb

3) amenity •   • c. lawyer

4) subsequent •   • d. prerequisite

5) requirement •   • e. convenience

4 각 문장의 빈칸에 가장 알맞은 단어를 보기에서 찾아 쓰세요.

> accordingly   assess   trial   interfere   register   submit

1) The terrorists are awaiting _____ in prison.

2) Whenever I pray to God, he responds _____.

3) The test is designed to _____ academic achievement.

4) You have to _____ the document by August, 14.

5) Today is the last day that I can _____ for the event.

Answer Key
1. (1) c. lawyer (2) b. superb (3) e. convenience (4) a. next (5) d. prerequisite
2. (1) trial (2) accordingly (3) assess (4) submit (5) register

Day 19 교육 Education 239

Let's Speak

Unit 1

Carol Your English has become quite **fluent**.
Allie Really? Maybe it's because I've kept watching soap operas at home. I watch them without subtitles since it might **interfere** with listening. It is a kind of a **trial** drama. The main characters are **attorneys**, so the conversations are very **coherent**.
Someone Could you be quiet?

Unit 2

Allie I studied in an **institute** in the Philippines for 3 months.
Monica I heard that the institutes there have great **amenities**.
Allie It differs between institutes. The institute where I studied didn't have good amenities, and it had very strict **discipline**. If you violated the rules, you were likely to be **dismissed**. So it was good that they **assessed** our academic achievements every week.

Unit 3

Yang The manager's kin gave me the tickets for the performance of an **outstanding** artist. The **admission** is free. You can go there with your friend tomorrow.
Allie Oh, thanks. But why aren't you going?
Yang I have another part-time job tomorrow. I have to work hard to earn money in order to **register** for the **subsequent** semester.
Allie Did you save a lot?
Yang I think I can concentrate only on studying when I get back to China. Then I might be able to receive a **scholarship**.

Unit 4

Allie The application deadline for a visa **extension** is in two days.
Monica How could you do nothing about it until now?
Allie I've been considering whether to stay or go back.
Monica You will have to **submit** the documents via mail because visit applications must be closed by now. A certificate from an **authorized** school is one of the **requirements**. Read the instructions carefully and complete the application form **accordingly**.

Day 20

미래 Future

Preview

- ☐ kidnap
- ☐ preliminary
- ☐ archaeology
- ☐ terrain
- ☐ alter
- ☐ immense
- ☐ inherit
- ☐ designate
- ☐ impose
- ☐ reside
- ☐ firm
- ☐ diploma
- ☐ prestige
- ☐ faculty
- ☐ endeavor
- ☐ cram
- ☐ discard
- ☐ seal
- ☐ spacious
- ☐ conceive

Unit 01 딸은 아버지를 닮아간다

LET'S STUDY

kidnap
[kídnæp]
동 납치하다, 유괴하다
(= abduct)

kidnap a woman 여성을 납치하다
kidnap children 아이들을 납치하다

The suspect has kidnapped a woman three times.
그 용의자는 여자를 세 번이나 납치했다.

There is a criminal gang that kidnaps children.
아이들을 납치하는 범죄 조직이 있다.

preliminary
[prilímənèri]
형 예비의
(= preparatory)
명 예비 행위

a **preliminary** research 예비 조사
a **preliminary** test 예비 시험

I've already conducted some preliminary research.
나는 벌써 어느 정도의 예비 조사를 했다.

All the applicants have to take the preliminary test.
모든 지원자들은 예비 시험을 쳐야 한다.

archaeology
[à:rkiálədʒi]
명 고고학

▶ archaeologist
명 고고학자

Egyptian **archaeology** 이집트 고고학
Maya **archaeology** 마야 고고학

We are all fascinated by Egyptian archaeology.
우리 모두는 이집트 고고학에 매료되어 있다.

This book is an easy guide to Maya archaeology.
이 책은 마야 고고학의 쉬운 안내서이다.

terrain
[təréin]
명 지형, 지세
(= landform)

flat **terrain** 평평한 지형
rough **terrain** 험한 지세

From tomorrow, we can finally walk on flat terrain.
내일부터는 드디어 평평한 지형에서 걸을 수 있다.

This mountain is notorious for its rough terrain.
이 산은 험한 지세로 악명이 높다.

alter
[ɔ́:ltər]
동 바꾸다, 달라지다

▶ alteration
명 변경, 개조

alter a fact 사실을 바꾸다
alter a plan 계획을 바꾸다

Nothing can alter the fact that you lied to me.
그 무엇도 네가 내게 거짓말을 했다는 사실을 바꿀 수는 없다.

I won't alter my plan to make a garden.
나는 정원을 만들기로 한 계획을 바꾸지 않을 것이다.

Unit 02 아직은 정착이 싫은

LET'S STUDY

immense
[iméns]
형 엄청난, 많은(= vast)

immense wealth 엄청난 재산
immense damage 엄청난 손해

Shawn used his immense wealth to help the poor.
숀은 가난한 사람들을 돕는데 그의 엄청난 재산을 사용했다.
The storm caused immense damage to many houses.
그 폭풍은 많은 집에 엄청난 손해를 입혔다.

inherit
[inhérit]
동 상속받다, 물려받다

▶ inheritance
명 유산; 유전

inherit a fortune 거금을 상속받다
inherit a disease 질병을 물려받다

Tony will inherit a fortune from his uncle.
토니는 삼촌으로부터 거금을 상속받을 것이다.
Clair inherited the disease from her mother.
클레어는 어머니에게서 그 질병을 물려받았다.

designate
[dézignit]
동 지명하다, 가리키다
형 지정된

▶ designation
명 지명, 지정

designate A as one's heir A를 상속자로 지정하다
designate A as a guardian A를 후견인으로 지정하다

Mr. Holman designated his nephew as his heir.
홀만 씨는 그의 조카를 상속자로 지정했다.
I designated Karen as a guardian for my children.
나는 카렌을 내 아이들을 위한 후견인으로 지정했다.

impose
[impóuz]
동 부과하다(= levy); 강요하다(= force)

impose a tax on ~에 세금을 부과하다
impose a penalty on ~에 처벌을 가하다

The government imposes high taxes on cigarettes.
정부는 담배에 높은 세금을 부과한다.
We need to impose severe penalties on drug dealers.
우리는 마약 밀매상에게 가혹한 처벌을 해야 한다.

reside
[rizáid]
동 거주하다, 살다 (= live)

reside in a village 마을에 거주하다
reside in an apartment 아파트에 거주하다

A small number of young men reside in this village.
적은 수의 젊은 사람들이 이 마을에 거주한다.
Most of my friends reside in apartments.
대부분의 내 친구들은 아파트에 거주한다.

Unit 03 모니카의 꿈

LET'S STUDY

firm
[fəːrm]

- 명 회사(= company)
- 형 단호한
- 동 단단하게 하다
- 부 단호하게

a design **firm** 디자인 회사
a law **firm** 법률 회사

Grace started a design firm with her friends.
그레이스는 친구들과 디자인 회사를 창업했다.
Billy is an attorney at the best law firm in town.
빌리는 도시 최고의 법률 회사에 근무하는 변호사이다.

diploma
[diplóumə]

- 명 학위(= degree), 졸업장

a **diploma** in economics 경제학 학위
a **diploma** in journalism 언론학 학위

I will earn my diploma in economics within two years.
나는 경제학 학위를 2년 내에 딸 것이다.
Kate got a diploma in journalism to become a reporter.
케이트는 기자가 되기 위해 언론학 학위를 받았다.

prestige
[prestíːdʒ]

- 명 명문; 고급

▶ prestigious
　형 명성 있는

a **prestige** school 명문 학교
a **prestige** item 고급 물품

St. Clair is one of the many prestige schools.
성 클레어는 많은 명문 학교들 중 하나이다.
This shop only deals in prestige items.
이 가게는 고급 물품만을 취급한다.

faculty
[fǽkəlti]

- 명 교수진(= professors), 교직원(= staff)

an excellent **faculty** 훌륭한 교수진
a **faculty** meeting 교직원 회의

The biggest merit of our school is its excellent faculty.
우리 학교의 가장 큰 장점은 훌륭한 교수진이다.
The next faculty meeting is scheduled on July 23.
다음 교직원 회의는 7월 23일로 예정되어 있다.

endeavor
[endévər]

- 명 노력
- 동 노력하다(= exert)

every **endeavor** 모든 노력
human **endeavor** 인간의 노력

Larry made every endeavor to make me a star.
래리는 나를 스타로 만들기 위해 모든 노력을 다 했다.
The human endeavor for immortality will never stop.
불멸을 향한 인간의 노력은 절대 멈추지 않을 것이다.

Unit 04 앨리의 미래

LET'S STUDY

cram
[kræm]
- 통 채워 넣다, 밀어 넣다 (= stuff)

cram A into a room 방에 A를 채워 넣다
cram A into a week 주중에 A를 끼워 넣다

The old woman crammed so much junk into her room.
그 나이든 여자는 방을 많은 잡동사니로 채워 넣었다.
I have to cram my personal training into this week.
나는 이번 주에 개인 훈련 수업을 끼워 넣어야 한다.

discard
[diskɑ́:rd]
- 통 버리다, 없애다 (= throw away)
- 명 포기; 폐기

discard clothes 옷을 버리다
discard an idea 생각을 버리다

Julie decided to discard all the clothes in her closet.
줄리는 옷장에 있는 옷을 전부 버리기로 결심했다.
I discarded the idea of buying the car.
나는 그 차를 사겠다는 생각을 버렸다.

seal
[si:l]
- 통 밀봉하다, 꽉 닫다 (= lock)
- 명 봉인; 도장 (= stamp)

seal a box 상자를 밀봉하다
seal a hole 구멍을 메우다

Adam and Brian sealed the boxes with tape.
아담과 브라이언은 그 상자들을 테이프로 밀봉했다.
Mrs. Robinson helped me seal the hole in my skirt.
로빈슨 부인은 내 치마의 구멍을 메우는 데 도움을 주셨다.

spacious
[spéiʃəs]
- 형 공간이 넓은 (= roomy)

a **spacious** house 넓은 집
a **spacious** kitchen 넓은 주방

We can buy a spacious house in the countryside.
우리는 시골에서 넓은 집을 살 수 있다.
A spacious kitchen is a dream of every house wife.
넓은 주방은 모든 가정 주부들의 꿈이다.

conceive
[kənsí:v]
- 통 상상하다; 임신하다
- ▶ conceivable
  형 상상할 수 있는, 생각할 수 있는

conceive of a future 미래를 상상하다
conceive a baby 아기를 임신하다

It's hard for me to conceive of a future without friends.
친구들이 없는 미래를 상상하는 건 어렵다.
Dr. Smith is helping those who want to conceive a baby.
스미스 박사는 임신을 원하는 사람들을 돕고 있다.

Review Test

1 다음 단어의 뜻을 고르세요.

1) conceive   a. 납치하다   b. 상상하다

2) prestige   a. 명문   b. 회사

3) impose   a. 상속받다   b. 부과하다

4) discard   a. 버리다   b. 거주하다

5) terrain   a. 지형   b. 교수진

2 각 문장에서 밑줄 친 부분에 해당하는 뜻을 포함한 단어를 보기에서 찾아 쓰세요.

> preliminary   spacious   seal   archaeology   designate   endeavor

1) 넓은 집으로 이사 가고 싶다.   (   )

2) 입학하려면 정말 노력해야 해!   (   )

3) 이미 예비 조사는 완벽히 했어.   (   )

4) 친척이 그를 상속자로 지명했어.   (   )

5) 대학에서 고고학을 전공하고 싶을 정도였어.   (   )

Answer Key

1. (1) b. 상상하다 (2) a. 명문 (3) b. 부과하다 (4) a. 버리다 (5) a. 지형
2. (1) spacious (2) endeavor (3) preliminary (4) designate (5) archaeology

3 각 단어를 유의어와 연결하세요.

1) immense •   • a. stuff

2) firm •   • b. abduct

3) kidnap •   • c. live

4) reside •   • d. vast

5) cram •   • e. company

4 각 문장의 빈칸에 가장 알맞은 단어를 보기에서 찾아 쓰세요.

> alter   seal   diploma   faculty   designate   inherit

1) I will earn my _____ in economics within two years.

2) Nothing can _____ the fact that you lied to me.

3) Tony will _____ a fortune from his uncle.

4) The biggest merit of our school is its excellent _____.

5) Mrs. Robinson helped me _____ the hole in my skirt.

Answer Key
1. (1) d. vast (2) e. company (3) b. abduct (4) c. live (5) a. stuff
2. (1) diploma (2) alter (3) inherit (4) faculty (5) seal

Let's Speak

Unit 1

Allie Since you are a woman, what will happen if you are **kidnapped** while traveling alone?

Carol I've already done thorough **preliminary** research. I loved Egypt so much that I even wanted to major in **archaeology** at university. It's been my dream to cross the desert. One of the attractions is the fact that the wind **alters** its **terrain** constantly, so it's hard to find the route.

Allie Good luck to you!

Unit 2

Monica Julio is going to **inherit immense** wealth. One of his kin **designated** him as an heir.

Julio Monica must have told you. But I gave it up.

Allie Why?

Julio The money is not much if I consider the tax **imposed** on the inheritance. Above all, there was a condition that I have to **reside** in my hometown for the rest of my life.

Unit 3

Allie You are going back to your country after this language course, right?

Monica No, I came here to live. It's better to get a **diploma** here to work in a design **firm** in England. There is a **prestige** fashion school. It also has an excellent **faculty**. I need to make every **endeavor** in order to enter the school.

Unit 4

Yang You **crammed** all the odds and ends. Can I **discard** these?

Allie They are all precious to me. I'll **seal** the box up and put it here. I really want to move into a **spacious** house.

Yang If you become successful, you can definitely do it. Allie, what's your dream?

Allie I want to speak English well and enter a good company.

Yang I mean your real dream.

Allie I meant it. Actually, I haven't really **conceived** of a specific future yet. It's not too late to seek it from now, right?

INDEX

INDEX

A

abundant	147
accommodate	153
accordingly	237
account	125
accrue	125
accumulate	69
acid	53
acquaintance	113
adept	105
admission	235
advance	161
advent	175
afford	113
agenda	165
aid	185
alert	129
alter	243
alternative	87
amenity	233
annual	173
anonymous	201
anticipate	223
antidote	199
antiseptic	69
apparatus	185
apparent	115
appeal	77
apply	189
appreciate	149
archaeology	243
arrest	89
artificial	99
assassinate	103
assault	129
assemble	55
assess	233
asset	105
assign	41
assist	159
astonish	225
attempt	141
attorney	231
authorize	237
awkward	79

B

bankrupt	189
barter	45
beverage	223
blend	141
boast	219
breakthrough	177
breeding	123
brisk	175
budget	173
bulk	127

C

capacity	111
capture	213
casualty	185
charge	77
charitable	41
cheat	139
chronic	67
circumstance	199
clash	135
coherent	231
coincidence	29
commemorate	221
commence	165
commit	195
committee	51
commodity	111
compatible	161
compensate	115

complement	223
compliment	79
comply	75
conceal	139
concede	43
conceive	249
conflict	43
congestion	221
conglomerate	175
conscience	33
consent	29
conservative	101
consider	207
constrain	117
consumption	45
contagious	63
contaminate	53
continual	43
contract	21
contrary	211
convention	187
convert	101
cooperate	51
corrupt	41
costly	65
costume	219
courteous	21
coverage	115
cram	249
criminal	129
cripple	149
critic	197
culprit	137
curb	225
curtail	175
customary	75

D

deadly	185
delinquent	135
depose	211
deposit	21
designate	245
destination	147
detergent	15
diagnose	99
dialect	213
diameter	221
dimension	55
diminish	161
diploma	247
discard	249
discipline	233
discriminate	189
dismiss	233
display	51
dispose	65
dispute	225
distress	117
district	27
divert	141
domestic	163
dull	31
durable	55

E

edible	105
effective	77
eliminate	53
embrace	19
emerge	39
emit	53
enclose	41
encounter	113
encourage	91

INDEX

encroach	171
endeavor	247
enroll	91
entail	91
enthusiasm	81
entitle	195
eradicate	89
erect	183
erode	53
erroneous	75
estimate	173
evidence	195
evident	65
exceed	147
excel	149
exclusive	151
execute	209
exhausted	27
exorbitant	75
expedition	103
expenditure	45
expense	189
exploit	33
extension	237
extent	45
extract	69
extraordinary	91
extravagant	15
extreme	91

F

fabric	159
faculty	247
fare	171
fasten	147
fatigue	129
feast	223
fertilizer	89
figure	201
financial	151
fine	89
firm	247
firsthand	163
flavor	141
flaw	43
flourish	209
fluent	231
forbid	15
forecast	87
forge	21
foster	187
fragile	31
fragrant	69
frugal	125
frustrated	199
fund	187
fundamental	177
furnish	19

G

genetically	111
genuine	39
glance	39
guarantee	175

H

hectic	93
hostage	103
hygiene	185

I

identity	197
immense	245
immoral	139
impair	149
impartial	137

implore	211	lodge	15
impose	245		
impressive	201	**M**	
improper	123		
improvise	219	mandatory	31
inauguration	209	manipulate	77
inclement	87	margin	127
indifferent	117	medieval	207
infrastructure	161	merge	213
inherit	245	merit	41
inquire	99	modest	79
inspire	197	monetary	33
institute	233	monitor	151
insurance	115		
interfere	231	**N**	
interpret	135		
intricate	195	negligible	17
invaluable	149	negotiate	81
investigate	195	nocturnal	89
		nominate	93
J		notable	43
		notify	15
jeopardize	103	nutrition	67
K		**O**	
keen	117	obsolete	45
kidnap	243	obstruct	199
kin	33	ominous	63
		operate	57
L		oppress	209
		ordinance	165
laboratory	197	outstanding	235
lag	219	overcome	27
launch	127	overseas	81
lawsuit	177	ownership	163
legendary	201		
legislation	93		
livelihood	153		
loan	125		

INDEX

P

paramount	17
pastime	79
patch	159
pension	173
permit	223
persist	177
perspiration	105
pious	101
pledge	139
plentiful	141
ponder	17
portrait	189
post	17
postpone	87
potential	163
predominant	93
preliminary	243
premium	115
prescribe	63
preserve	151
prestige	247
proclaim	183
prohibit	151
prolong	17
prominent	197
property	113
proponent	165
provoke	135
proximity	39

Q

qualification	99
quality	57

R

rational	199
readily	31
reasonable	55
recession	171
reconcile	225
recruit	29
redundant	111
reform	187
refrain	101
register	235
reliance	139
renewal	67
representative	201
requirement	237
reside	245
resident	29
restrict	165
retail	127
retreat	183
retrieve	129
reverse	117
riot	171
rural	207

S

sanitation	19
scenic	207
scheme	211
scholarship	235
scrutinize	137
seal	249
sensitive	163
sentence	137
shabby	123
shrink	77
sluggish	33
smuggle	51

soothe	69
sophisticated	75
souvenir	51
sovereignty	213
spacious	249
spectator	221
spur	159
stain	57
stale	111
stamina	159
sterile	99
stipulation	21
stir	105
stock	57
strike	171
stroll	207
struggle	153
submerge	153
submit	237
subordinate	221
subsequent	235
subsidize	173
subsist	123
substantial	81
suburb	19
successive	27
successor	211
supervise	31
surplus	67
surrender	183
susceptible	67
sustain	209

T

tariff	127
temporary	81
terminal	63
terrain	243
testify	137

torrential	87
transform	123
transition	187
trespass	113
trial	231
trigger	183
trivial	63
turbulence	147

U

unanimous	29
undergo	65
union	213
utility	19

V

vacancy	27
vague	177
vanish	65
variation	93
vehicle	153
venture	103
versatile	79
victim	135
vigorous	39
violate	101
vogue	219
voluntary	57
vomit	225

W

wholesale	55
widen	161
withdraw	125